HOW
TO
CHOOSE
A
COLLEGE
MAJOR

HOW TO CHOOSE A COLLEGE MAJOR

Linda Landis Andrews

VGM Career Horizons
NTC/Contemporary Publishing Company

Library of Congress Cataloging-in-Publication Data

Andrews, Linda Landis.
    How to choose a college major / Linda Landis Andrews.
      p. cm.
    ISBN 0-8442-8120-4
    1. College majors—United States.   I. Title.
  LB2361.5.145 1997
  378.1′9422—dc21   97-14985
                         CIP

Published by VGM Career Horizons
An imprint of NTC/Contemporary Publishing Company
4255 West Touhy Avenue, Lincolnwood (Chicago), Illinois 60646-1975 U.S.A.
Manufactured in the United States of America
International Standard Book Number: 0-8442-8120-4

15   14   13   12   11   10   9   8   7   6   5   4   3   2   1

Contents

Tasks to Get You to Your Major 69

**Descriptions of Majors from College
        Catalogues 85**

Foreword

Understanding that you have more choices than you thought possible is the beginning of wisdom. And freedom. The poet was wrong. To travel down one road does not mean excluding the others. You still have to carry the same backpack.

   Some will tell you that college is "the time of your life." They envy your youth, your energy, your choices. They have forgotten how burdensome those can be without a compass. Imagine your choices, cast your net far and wide, celebrate your decisions, and, as I tell my daughter every time she approaches a new journey, "Remember, your job is to have fun."

HOW
TO
CHOOSE
A
COLLEGE
MAJOR

The Important Question of Your Major

"What are you majoring in?" This question bounces around campus, in the cafeteria, at basketball games, in movie lines, every place where students gather. It's a nagging, incessant question, roiling like a wave over the quadrangle. The supremely confident students have sure-fire, too-quick answers, but others are more tentative:

> "I was a nursing major but now I'm in kinesiology."
>
> "I don't know, I'm still deciding."
>
> "My father thinks I should be in engineering but I'm more interested in history."
>
> "I'm switching to poli sci. I'm tired of making myself miserable with business courses I'm not interested in."

These responses are typical. Some students quickly decide on a major and stick to it as if bonded with a strong adhe-

1

sive all the way through college. But for many students, choosing a major is a difficult and sometimes agonizing decision.

The decision is difficult because most students don't have sufficient information to make an appropriate choice. Students lack information in four areas:

1. Personal information about themselves: interests, aptitude, motivation, and values

2. Knowledge of what particular majors mean

3. Information on how majors interact with careers

4. What skills they will need after graduation

This information is available but it takes time to gather. This book is intended as a guide to help you find all the information you will need to make an intelligent decision in choosing a college major. When you are finished gathering the information, you will choose a major based on insight, not guesswork.

An Important Decision That Can Save Years and Dollars

Why is six years the average time an American student spends in college today? Many are working and going to school at the same time. But an overwhelming factor is students changing majors midstream. Millions of dollars are spent each year on majors that students change before graduation day. Declaring a major without sufficient preparation often leads to worry, frustration, loss of sleep, discouragement, and a feeling of having to start all over again. The saying is shopworn but apt: Look before you leap.

The cost of this confusion continues to rise as college costs escalate. The average increase in college cost is running greater than the rate of inflation. Annual costs at some elite private schools exceed $30,000. The expenses for in-state residents at some first-tier public universities have passed $10,000 yearly.

Even if money is not a concern, the possibility of spending that money and the student having no meaningful job upon graduation worries many parents. Add to this a year or more of taking courses in a wrong major and the costs go up. This is an enormous waste of time and energy and can be avoided.

By reading this book and following the suggestions you will save yourself much unneeded confusion and countless dollars. Time and energy are precious commodities, not to be wasted. College is a time to meet new people, explore ideas, grow as a human being. This period should not be spoiled by needless anxiety about your major. Information is power, and it is within your grasp. Be patient with yourself on this journey of discovery and you will gain much along the way.

One of the important skills you will learn in college is how to analyze problems. Consider choosing a major an exercise in problem solving. Heads of many corporations today say they are looking for people who can solve problems. They also want people who can communicate effectively, get along with others, and reach goals through team activities.

Your number one goal now is to solve the problem of choosing a major. How you do this can serve as a blueprint for other important decisions in the years ahead.

Problem-Solving Styles—A Trip to the Video Store

Your ability to solve problems is affected by many factors including temperament, birth order, how problems were solved in your family, and how much time you take to analyze a problem. Think about what happens on a trip to the video store with friends. When you get there, a dizzying array of titles screams out from categories such as foreign films, new releases, dramas, horror stories, how tos, exercise videos, and so on. You strain to remember what you've heard about the different films. Much of your impressions will come from previous advertising, word of mouth, reviews. You browse, see what's available, read the film jackets, ask attractive strangers near you what they recommend, and finally make a decision.

Before anyone takes offense at the comparison of choosing a major and choosing a rental movie, consider the process of confusion, investigation, and conclusion. You're confused about a major, you ask people about subjects, and you reach a decision. And one of the tenets of good problem solving is to remember that few decisions are irrevocable. If you don't like the movie, you turn off the VCR and vow never to rent another one starring Jim Carrey. In the same way, if you choose a major and the first few courses are disappointing, you can regroup.

What a Major Means Today

At most colleges and universities, a major means an area of specialization that you will pursue through 24 to 40 courses. A list of typical majors and their descriptions follows in Chapter 5. In Chapter 6, you will see a list of courses required in some majors. A course may carry any number of credit hours but most courses carry three credits and some four. Each major has a certain amount of required courses and then there are elective courses, courses you choose on your own within the field. These give you a degree of freedom, and students usually enjoy the selection process. A theater major, for instance, might take Improvisation as an elective, besides the required courses such as Stage Design, Acting, and History of Theater.

A minor is your secondary field of interest and requires fewer courses. You also have the option of choosing a double major.

The Changing Face of Majors

Today's major isn't what it used to be. Technology has revolutionized research that you will be doing in your major, making information on any subject both more accessible and broader in scope. A desire for flexibility in courses of study has made the interdisciplinary majors, those in which you study two or more subjects, very popular. Majors have changed enormously in the past thirty years and will continue to change.

The field of library science is a good example of the enormous change wrought by technology. In the old days, students found information through Melvil Dewey's decimal system. They pulled out wooden drawers filled with cards giving the names of authors, book titles, and codes indicating where the books could be found on shelves. Today, students sit in front of a computer screen, hit keys, and let search engines such as Yahoo! do the research. The transition isn't complete, but as full-text retrieval of documents becomes widely available, the role of libraries will change even more. In the future, librarians will be the cyberspace experts, guiding students through the maze of electronic information. As a result of this change, library science education programs have closed, leaving only sixty that offer an undergraduate major in library science.

The revolution has not happened the way it had been predicted, however. Not long ago people were predicting the disappearance of libraries beginning in the year 2000, to be replaced by digital sources of information. Instead, libraries have changed to keep up with the advances of technology with librarians leading the charge through cyberspace.

Similarly, the computer has revolutionized graphic arts. Artists are now trained to move easily between print design and CD-ROM, text and illustration, photo and illustration. Rather than stifling creativity, the computer has enhanced it, allowing artists to cross boundaries between media.

Graphic artists can no longer create merely with what they know, relying on their inner creativity and intuition. Technology keeps advancing their field with new programs, new ways to create. In a very fundamental way, their life work has been changed by technology.

New Majors Have Been Added

And many new majors have been added. Thirty years ago few colleges offered a major in women's studies; today most offer at least a minor in women's studies. As the culture changes students are interested in new subjects. Professors, intrigued with researching a new area, suggest a new course. More research is conducted and a few more courses are added. The evolution is completed when the subject area is offered as a major. In Chapter 7, you will find descriptions of majors such as toy design and golf management that have been created as interest in these subjects has evolved.

Competition and Acceleration

Because so many more people are going to college now than in your parents' day, the number of people holding college degrees has increased. To excel and compete, many people feel that graduate school is necessary. In the competition for jobs, they think an advanced degree puts people at an advantage. A large number of people go to graduate school because they find their options limited after college. They also feel that they want to progress further in knowledge than what they learned with an undergraduate degree.

For these reasons, the choice of what you major in is not as important as it was in years past as long as you like the subject and are motivated to study it. One popular notion holds that a college degree today has as much worth as high school did in the 1940s. Many top jobs of the future will require a master's degree.

In the area of doctorates, a different law of demand and supply is working. There are so many Ph.D.s today competing to teach at the college level, for instance, that teaching at the high school level has become a consideration for some of these job seekers.

The World Has Shrunk

The rise of markets in Europe, Latin America, and the Far East has increased competition for jobs, even for college-educated people. A United States firm in South

America recruited a recent American college graduate to help establish a chain of movie theaters there. He was sent to London for training in the movie theater management business and now is working in Chile managing multiplex movie houses. A big-city mayor hired a team of recent college graduates to develop trade relations with Central America. Highly skilled in presentations, they travel and work 60-hour weeks promoting trade for the city.

Building business abroad is a major focus of the American economy. Increasingly, many American companies want their employees to have experience working abroad so that they are comfortable in emerging markets. But this has a downside for graduates looking for work. American college graduates find themselves in competition with people from other countries in securing jobs with American firms.

Multiculturalism—understanding and appreciating reality in different cultures—has affected many majors. Also affecting majors has been a distrust of relying on the information provided solely by "dead white men." There has been a push to discover and appreciate work of all people and to celebrate the differences among people.

The Computer Revolution

Not only has the number of majors increased, the way majors are taught also has changed. Most today rely on computer literacy. Computer labs, open twenty-four hours a day, are available on every campus. Certain computer labs are designed for specific departments with specialized software. Students are required to learn the computer skills they will need to complete research in their major.

Futurists are predicting virtual universities where some students will complete a large part of their educations in front of a computer screen. In this future scenario, colleges will team up and students hypothetically might be able to take a course at a school in Minnesota, one from Boston, and the rest from their original campus, all via cyberspace. Working professionals, after a busy day at the office, will be able to get advanced degrees in the evening at home.

Trends Affect Popularity of Majors

Students and parents see trends in the media and certain majors get "hot." The herd mentality takes over and certain fields are hard to get into. "The popularity of some college majors has changed in ten years," said Gretchen W. Rigol, the College Board's executive director of admissions and guidance services. "Health-related fields are now the top choice of college-bound seniors, ahead of business, which is in second place. Ten years ago, 23 percent of students planned to major in business and 13 percent in health. Today, business is 13 percent and health 19 percent," she said.

The Connection Between Majors and Careers

Majors today are more tightly tied to the prospect of value than ever before. Parents want to know what their offspring are going to "do" after graduation. It is hard to imagine in this highly competitive world, but thirty years ago people went to college only vaguely aware of how what they learned in college was going to have an effect on what they did for a living. There were notable exceptions: engineering, speech therapy, nursing. The emphasis, however, was on "going to college." Most people who went to college received a broad education. This breadth of knowledge provided them with a way of thinking, an educated perception. At college they learned about existentialism, the Supreme Court, Ayn Rand. Today colleges increasingly are under pressure to prepare students for careers.

As a result of this new focus, interaction with the outside world is prevalent. Many working professionals teach a class, bringing their special expertise to campus. Students are encouraged to take multiple internships or cooperative education jobs before they reach the job market to have a more realistic view of what they will be doing. In the past, companies took people who were college educated and trained them. Today, much more of the responsibility of training people falls on the colleges and universities. The world seems to be moving too quickly to delay career awareness until after graduation.

Declaring Your Major

Early Decision Makers

A few students know early what interests them. Ed Cook was raised near Boston, the land of early American history, the Pilgrims, Lexington and Concord. "History was something I clearly liked in junior high and it was always the thing that fascinated me in high school. It was a natural progression to a major in college."

For his senior paper at Harvard he researched the early 18th century social history of a New England town, Dedham, Massachusetts. The town had well-preserved minutes of town meetings and tax lists. A particularly effective historical society had collected papers and diaries, a bonanza for an historian. Cook earned his doctorate in early American history at Johns Hopkins

University and now teaches at the University of Chicago. He has written a book, *The Fathers of the Towns: Leadership and Community Development in 18th Century New England.* His lifelong ambition started in junior high and never wavered.

Most students need more time, realizing that they can't possibly know what each major entails, what they're good at, or how the workplace is viewing a particular major today. It may surprise you to know that some people don't discover a subject they feel passionate about until they are in their fifties or sixties. Trying to know at eighteen is asking a great deal of yourself.

When Are Majors Declared?

At most schools majors are declared in spring of sophomore year. During the first two years of college, you should

1. take a variety of classes
2. talk to professors
3. compare ideas about majors with upperclass students
4. visit the career counseling office
5. attend seminars on majors and career paths
6. talk to working professionals about their majors in college
7. think about a double major or a minor that complements the major

During the summer between sophomore and junior year, you might worry about the "major" decision you have made, probably second-guessing yourself a couple of times. You still have time. In first semester junior year, courses in the major will help you determine if this is the area that will hold your interest.

How Do I Declare One?

Your college catalogue will indicate the specific way that you declare a major. Usually it involves contacting the department and formally declaring the major in writing. Some departments require application and a certain grade point average.

After you declare a major, you will probably be assigned an advisor in the department. At large schools students frequently reach graduation without ever seeing an advisor. This is unfortunate because advisors can be very helpful. They are able to keep you on track with required courses in order to graduate on time and check the transferability of summer school credit from another college.

Most schools require that a substantial number of your final credit hours be earned at the school from which you plan to graduate. If you spend time abroad under the auspices of the school from which you intend to graduate, the year counts as in residence.

The Realities of College Today

Newsweek magazine reports that there are 2,200 four-year colleges and universities enrolling 8.8 million students. These institutions are called "the primary trainer of the nation's professional, managerial, technical elites." Of this number, 5.2 million people are full-time undergraduates. Each of these people has to come to terms with choosing a major. Some will be graduated without a clue as to what they can do with their majors. Others, like you, will have done the necessary homework to find

1. What interests you
2. Your talents
3. Your values
4. How to match these with a career

The goal is to choose a major wisely and not spend unnecessary extra time and money in college.

Bureaucracy and Paperwork

If you let it, the bureaucracy of colleges and universities will eat you up alive. All the forms you must fill out, the deadlines you must meet, and the people you must talk to about your particular situation are daunting. After a while, however, they become part of life. As a student facing them for the first time, you may be overwhelmed. It will get better as you learn shortcuts for getting through the red tape. Tackling the bureaucracy is definitely a skill you learn in college that will help you on the outside.

Remedy One. People skills are what will guide you through the bureaucracy of college. These skills do not come automatically. You have to learn how to talk to clerical staff, teaching assistants, lecturers, financial aid personnel, counselors, and professors. If you are too shy to ask for permission to join a class that you need, now is the time to build that skill. Start by asking people for things you don't care about. When nothing is at stake, you can try different approaches. Are people more apt to help you when you are bold? polite? indifferent? menacing? Try out what works for you.

Remedy Two. Attention to details is a helpful habit. If you remember to dot every i, cross every t, and keep copies of everything, you will be way ahead of the game. When you talk to people on the phone, be sure to write down the date and the name of the person who gave you the information. Speaking of keeping copies—be sure to keep either hard copies or disk copies of papers you submit in class. Too often papers get lost. Even professors lose grade books and have to request that each student bring in graded papers already handed back. Years after a course, you may need a copy of your paper for different reasons: to refresh the memory of a professor writing a letter of recommendation for you, or to show work you have researched to a prospective employer.

Remedy Three. A sense of humor is also beneficial in dealing with bureaucracy. If you can laugh at the stupid things that happen to you, you will be less likely to crash and burn. Laughing will help you put things in perspective.

The Rule of Replacement. Remember the rule of replacement: Whatever is the crisis in your life today will be replaced by another crisis six months in the future.

Registration

Majors have been lost and won on the basis of what courses were available at the time of registration. Many schools have telephone registration today, but usually upperclasspeople, members of clubs, the honors college, and athletes get first choice. If you can't get into the prerequisites for your major or can't fill your schedule with the requisites for your major, it begins to feel a bit futile. As with the many other lessons students learn in college, motivation is the key. Find out how you can get priority for registration. You may have to join a club. When you can't get into a class, talk to the professor or e-mail her. Beg. You are not going to be a math major if you cannot get into Calculus I.

Getting the Best Instructors

On every campus tour a parent asks how many classes are taught by professors versus how many are taught by teaching assistants (TAs). The parents imagine that if more teaching is done by professors, their child will receive a better education. Not necessarily. Professors may be preoccupied with their research. Teaching assistants bring energy and newness to the job and frequently are more accessible than professors.

Whether it's a professor or a teaching assistant, getting the good ones for all your classes is the challenge. What does "good" mean? Generally it means relating well to students and being able to communicate with them. It means being fair in assignments and grading. It means being up-to-date in the field. Being taught well can make the difference between a grade of A or D. Or it can make the difference between your being excited about your major or discouraged. Shop around. At some schools the student government publishes a guide to the instructors with data gathered from students. Questionnaires ask students if the instructor grades fairly, about the workload, presentation style, and availability during office hours, and encourage students to write additional comments.

Remedy. Don't blindly sign up for a course without trying to find out about the instructor. Ask questions of upperclasspeople. See if the syllabus, the instructor's plan for the course, is on-line before the term begins. Usually the syllabus includes the instructor's policies regarding grading, plagiarism, and attendance, and what is expected of you for the course. Some include cartoons or ridiculous statements to make sure you are reading them. The syllabi of others are very formal. What most students care about in a course is substance, fairness in grading, and a clear sense of what is going on.

Grades and Withdrawals

Be sure you understand what factors will affect your grade. Handing in assignments late may lower your grade. Most instructors hate late papers. They also are not fond of hearing the reasons why papers are late or why you can't attend class. Some instructors don't care if you ever come to class; others take attendance and lower your grade if you exceed the specified absences spelled out in the syllabus. Policy varies enormously. Other instructors will not give you a good grade unless you have participated in class discussions. Try to imagine their situation: over the years they have heard all sorts of reasons why students can't do the work. It gets boring and repetitious for them. This does not mean they are unwilling to be helpful, but they can't help students avoid traffic court dates, retrieve work on the computer that gets lost in a power outage, or recover from pneumonia. Your grade will depend on your performance and it is in your best interest to understand what will be required. Just do it.

It is crucial to your grade point average to know the time period in which you can withdraw from a course. At some schools it's as long as six weeks; others have shaved it down to two weeks. Drop the course if you are behind and have little hope of catching up. You can make the time up in summer school.

Prerequisites

Most freshmen take introductory courses unless they have tested out of the required courses. Typically, this happens when a student has had a great deal of advanced preparation in high school, say four years of French and living with a French family for a term. Predictably, this person is much more likely to score highly and place out of French 101 than someone who doesn't know what a croissant is. The introductory courses freshman year will let you tread water while you investigate where each major leads.

Many times students get discouraged at this stage. The sections are sometimes very large, students are talking on their cellular phones during the lecture, and the class atmosphere feels like a sea of confusion rather than any real excitement about learning a new subject. Pay your dues—you have to take these lower-level courses as prerequisites for the upper-level, more intense courses that provide the excitement of a major.

Course Requirements

The school's catalogue lists the course requirements. For example, the catalogue of Grinnell College says this about the Latin American Studies major:

> Students examine Spanish-American cultures and societies, with work in at least three areas: language and literature, cultural history, and social sciences. Participation in a study program in Latin America is encouraged (see Off-Campus Study). In the senior research project and presentation, a student is expected to integrate the various components of his or her program in the analysis of a topic of special interest.

Then the catalogue will list what requirements are needed, specifically outlining where the credits—24 in this case—need to be gathered. The pages where this is listed for your major will become dog-eared from the many times you have to consult them.

Life Intrusions

Even the best-laid plans sometimes are upset. You might wait three hours to get connected to telephone registration. You might register for the course you need, start the course, and find that you just don't grasp the material. You might go to the tutors on campus, visit the professor during office hours, and find that nothing works. Almost everyone in college has had this experience. You may not be ready for this course yet.

Perhaps next term the material will be easier to grasp. Drop the course. Agony over studying isn't worth it. Summer school is tough because a whole term of material is condensed, for instance, from 16 weeks to 8 weeks. But staying in the course may discourage you too much from pursuing the major you have chosen.

Or let's say this is a particularly tough semester because of personal problems. College-age students have parents who are at middle age and may be facing their own turmoil: a health problem, loss of a job, divorce, job relocation. This is also the time when young people are forming new relationships, which are distracting. Consider how much stress you are under before you change majors. Your choice of major may be entirely appropriate, but the current course you are taking in it during this stressful time may be discouraging.

Shouldering the Cost

The high cost of college is a fact of life. Students used to be resigned to college costs thinking they would be compensated with higher-paying jobs. Now they are not so sure there will be a pot of gold at the end of the graduation line. A freshman at Northwestern interviewed on the "Today Show" said he got nervous every time he took a test or handed in a paper, knowing how much his education was costing and feeling the pressure. The pressure is pervasive. Students feel they must choose a major that will assure them of the ability to pay off their student loans. They feel pressured knowing how privileged they are to even be attending such an expensive institution.

Remedy One. Remember that time is on your side. You may have a great deal of debt, but you also are very young. You will have twenty-five years of productive work life to pay off student loans.

Remedy Two. Realize that your education will not end in school. In any career you have the option of adding skills that will benefit you through your paycheck. You will have the option of taking on new responsibilities to add to your own prosperity.

Remedy Three. Remember that the cost of education will rise. If recent history is an indicator, the cost of education will continue to go up. So you are taking advantage of the lowest possible expense.

Personal Success Tools

Build Decision-Making Skills

Learning how to make decisions of optimum benefit to you is a skill that will be helpful the rest of your days. You already have begun the steps in effective decision making. The evidence:

1. You have identified the challenge, searching for the best major for you.
2. You have started to gather information, reading this book and talking to others to be aware of your options.
3. You have not panicked and picked the first option that seemed feasible.

Becoming aware of how you have made decisions in the past is helpful. You have seen classmates and friends in the different types of ineffective decision-making modes:

1. accepting the first idea that presents itself
2. being easily persuaded by others
3. having no clear correlation between decision and goals
4. relying on faulty information

Obviously, you will be using the opposite tactics:

1. investigating several ideas before making a decision
2. being independent in thinking; not easily swayed by others

3. having a clear idea of goals and how decisions affect these

4. checking and rechecking information to be sure it is accurate

Information Is Power

One of the main tasks students perform at college is research. They conduct research in the library, on microfilm, on the Netscape. They investigate in the laboratory. They gather wisdom from faculty. Students are trained not to jump to early conclusions. Particularly in the case of choosing a major, you have to gather information. Most often when people are indecisive it's because they do not have enough information. Weighing the pros and cons of each interesting major is impossible if you don't have enough information to put on each side of the scale.

Bradford and Isaac: Contrasting Styles. Two freshmen are making out their sophomore year schedules at a large university. One, Bradford, has just pledged a fraternity and takes the advice of a junior in the frat house about what courses to take. The other, Isaac, talks to an advisor in his college about the distribution of credits required for graduation, studies the college catalogue to make sure he understands the course sequence, then double checks with the college advising office to make sure what he needs is being offered the following year. Isaac invests time and energy into getting the information. Now, Bradford may luck out, but who wants to rely on luck? Isaac also got a signed note from the advisor so that later he will have proof of what he was told and by whom. Isaac's funny that way. Whenever he gets information of any kind over the phone or in person he asks for the name of the person he's speaking with. And he keeps his notes.

Rules and requirements change regularly. You can receive five different pieces of information from five people in the same division of a college. Three may have been hired last week.

Majors change also. Industries regularly change what they are looking for in new college graduates. If you at least investigate beforehand what you are going to major in, the surprise of a new trend won't be as great.

When talking to people about majors, remember that everyone has a different basis for his or her opinion. Some people think a major is desirable only if it leads to making a lot of money. Others hold a very traditional view of what college should be. Parents sometimes are biased for or against what they majored in. Or they may feel that college isn't necessary because they didn't go. People have a bias based on their own experiences. Gathering many opinions will give you wisdom about a particular major. Just as in any range, the opinions at each end will be the extremes and the truth is likely to be somewhere in the middle.

The exciting part of your investigation is the learning curve. When you start out, you will know little, but bit by bit each piece of information will add to your heap until you will have amassed a great deal of savvy about the subject.

Some of the information will be contradictory. Perhaps an impression is out of date or not based on a wide enough sample. When two descriptions conflict, choose the opinion of the person who seems more reliable. And be careful of people spouting offhand comments that sound like the truth but aren't. Example: There are no jobs for English majors. This is completely false. Many students in Chapter 10, "Learning from Others," will tell you why.

Weighing Pros and Cons

Although it may take some time, a piece of paper with a line drawn down the middle and the word "Pros" in one column and "Cons" heading the other may clear up confusion. Visualization of the decision in this way promotes thinking in another way. Typical column items are:

Years in school required for this major

Difficulty of courses

Natural ability

Enjoyment of the subject

Motivation to study this subject

Value you put on this subject

Jobs available after graduation

Salary ranges

Cost of getting this degree

Maria's Story. Here's the chart of Maria, a student weighing the pros and cons of majoring in Physical Therapy:

Pros	Cons
Natural ability	Years in school required for this major
Motivation to study this subject	Difficulty of courses (not sure she can get good grades)

Enjoyment of the subject	Does not know anyone in the field
Jobs available after graduation	
Good pay	
Values worth of this subject	

Through research, Maria has learned that she will eventually need a master's degree and getting accepted into a program is difficult. As far as the difficulty of the courses is concerned, she needs to take prep courses before college. She must evaluate whether or not being a physical therapist means enough to her to struggle for the good grades. She needs a plan of action to be successful, leaving as little as possible to chance. Talking to recent graduates in physical therapy will be helpful in assessing whether her natural interest in helping people who have had strokes or other physical problems motivates her enough to work hard during the courses for the major.

Maria finds a physical therapist through her pharmacist uncle and spends a morning watching her interact with patients. She is impressed with how much the patients rely on the physical therapist to teach them how to rebuild their lives.

After talking with people on campus she realizes that every major is difficult and that physical therapy courses are probably no tougher than other disciplines. She decides to go for it.

Postscript: Today Maria has a master's in physical therapy and works in the professional offices of a suburban hospital.

Sean's Story. Sean comes from a family of cops. His uncles and father have told him that if he wants to go into law enforcement in the future, his options will be better with a college degree in Criminal Justice.

Sean's chart on the pros and cons of majoring in Criminal Justice is as follows:

Pros	*Cons*
Motivation to study this subject	Strong competition for jobs
Courses not too difficult	Lower salary
Enjoyment of the subject	Tied too closely to family

expectations
Natural ability
Family in law enforcement
Police scholarship available
Fits with his values

Although Sean is confident he can get through the program, he is not sure there will be a job for him when he finishes. Also, he feels as if he's considering this field because it is the only one he knows, through his family.

Postscript: Sean decided he did not have enough information to make a decision. He talked with a career counselor and several police officers who were not related to him. Still unsure, he decided to get training as an emergency medical technician (EMT), which involves 120 hours of classroom instruction plus 10 hours of internship in a hospital emergency room. He believes this will give him added exposure to police work in order to determine if he wants to major in criminal justice. Plus, he thinks it will be exciting.

Your Chart. Your chart of pros and cons will be extremely helpful in weighing your choices. Fill in as many benefits and negatives as you can. If you don't know the pros and cons, now is the time to find out. Make a chart for each major you are considering.

Pros and Cons Chart

Major:

Pros	Cons

Do You Have the Stamina to Complete Your Major?

Take into consideration whether you have enough interest in the major to plow through some uninteresting courses along with the exciting ones. Not all the courses will be enticing, but most will if you have made the right choice. Chapter 6 in this book reviews courses typical in each major.

Tactics for Staying on Course

Surviving in school and getting through the prerequisites requires the following:

1. Be patient with yourself.
2. Realize that there is no perfect way to get through college. The journey has its ups and downs like any other life journey.
3. Expect setbacks: a killer course, a broken ankle, a computer failure that wipes out a paper the night before it's due.
4. Develop your people and negotiating skills.
5. Keep hard or disk copies of every paper you submit.
6. Develop contacts in class whom you can call with questions about the material.
7. Tackle personal problems with the help of the Counseling Center.

9. Ask for help. Much more help is available on campuses than students ever use.

10. Vary your tasks every day and plan a social life. Staying with the books or the computer screen all the time will stunt a very important part of your growth.

Life in a New World— Talk to Strangers

A majority of students who go off to school for the first time have never experienced life outside of their families. New skills are required to successfully tackle the job of college.

A willingness to strike up conversations with strangers is important. All your life, people have been telling you not to talk to strangers, but in college many old ideas have to be discarded. A wealth of interesting people exist on every campus. A painless way to meet some of these people is by joining a club or other interest group on campus or in the nearby community.

A sense of community is very important to your well-being. The first few weeks on any campus can be daunting, especially with the swirl of unfamiliar classrooms, faces, and faculty greeting you. College administrators, alarmed by the increasing number of students who drop out during freshman year, offer orientation programs to help students make the transition from high school to college. Frequently, freshmen come to campus before school starts to meet new people and attend seminars on cultural diversity, date rape, alcohol awareness, and other social issues. With new freedom, students must make choices about how to manage their time and money, whom to socialize with, and how to succeed in their new environment.

Experiment, take chances, get out of your room and dorm. Be sure you explore all the campus facilities and activities that are available to you. Getting comfortable is a major task.

Forces That Sway the Major Decision

Old ideas or stereotypes about what a major means influence students' decisions about majors. A good example is accounting. In the past, accountants were considered "number crunchers" who had no personalities and never saw the light of day. That has all changed. Interaction with clients is considered highly important today in the field of accounting, and students majoring in this field must have good people skills. Also, many accountants find that a great deal of time is spent selling their expertise to gain new clients. Students who choose accounting today must develop their oral and written communication skills and their ability to be comfortable with people.

Every major has changed in the past twenty years because of changes in our society. Parents and students talk with astonishment about what they find out about majors after visiting several schools. And once people graduate, they must still keep up to date in their field through additional courses and seminars, or they will fall behind. So it's important to check on the majors that interest you to see what they actually mean today.

Talking with people on campus is the best way of finding out what a major means today. Gather printed material, especially the college catalogue, but do not rely on this. You must talk with people because the material may be out of date. Some of the courses listed may have been dropped since the last printing or may be offered only occasionally. A faculty may have voted just last week to change a major or a course, making the material you are reading incorrect.

Knowledgeable people are your guides to the territory. Talking with one or two isn't sufficient. You need to talk with students, admissions counselors, and, if possible, people in the department you are considering joining. Usually, these people are readily available and give talks during college visits. Go up to each one and talk, even if their talks are not about the major you are considering. This will give you experience in talking with professors and wider exposure than you had before to what different majors mean.

Developing Patience

Many students become unnecessarily impatient with themselves in the process of choosing a major. They become panicked when they see classmates in the senior year in high school confidently declaring what they are going to be doing for the rest of their lives. How can a high school senior know this? The employment gurus say that people will, on average, change their careers seven times in their lives. A nurse returns to school years later and gets a doctorate in theology because she wants to offer spirituality in medicine; a former fighter pilot in Vietnam goes into his family's retail business but sells it at age fifty to get a law degree. People happily evolve into much more than they were as college students. They grow.

Peer pressure, however, saps patience. It is distressing to see everyone running off with plans while you have none. The irony is that people who take time to figure out what they are going to do frequently are the ones who end up more secure in the long run. The problem with impatience is that it usually manifests itself in impatience with other people. Yet students need other people to help them find what major path they should follow.

Tips for Finding the Right Major for You

Staying focused on your search for a major involves being optimistic. Take nine optimism pills every morning. In addition, remember to:

1. Cheer your friends on as they choose their majors, but remember, their decisions don't have anything to do with you. Their decisions are interesting but irrelevant.

2. Set aside a time every week when you are going to think about your major, but don't obsess every day about the decision.

3. Get organized in your search. Keep a notebook especially for information about majors.

4. Notice how you make small decisions. Do you gather information and choose among several options? Or do you choose the first idea that comes to you? Obviously, if you're doing the latter, you aren't taking advantage of all your options.

5. Develop a sense of perspective. You aren't the first person who has had to choose a major, or who has had difficulty with the decision.

6. Keep looking for more information, more angles. These are speedy times and facts and trends change very quickly. Be alert to changes.

The End Is Worth It

Whatever major you choose, you will be better off than if you had never chosen one at all. College graduates today may start out in low-paying jobs but eventually become quite respectable, according to a study reported in *Business Week* magazine. The study, conducted by professors at Harvard and MIT, reported that while recent graduates may initially take low-paying jobs, by the time they are thirty they have joined middle-class ranks in salary. Presumably, college gives people the skills to improve their lot in life.

Who Am I? Time to Take Stock

Who are you? There are so many words that could be used to describe you. Are you spontaneous? quiet? adventuresome? studious? playful? determined? Knowing yourself is the ultimate education. The more you know about yourself, the easier the task of choosing a major that fits with your interests, your abilities, your values, your personal motivation. In this chapter, you will find ways of determining who you are.

Many factors contribute to who you are. A large part of you is determined by your genes (nature). Then the environment makes an impact (nurture). A current theory holds that even happiness may be determined by genes. According to this theory, happiness seems to be set, with people always returning to their preset happiness level. Other studies have sought to demonstrate that shyness or a set weight are inherited.

Many people feel that environment, what you are

exposed to as you grow, greatly determines who you will become. Understanding as much as you can about yourself, including heredity and environment, is an important task. In the area of choosing a college major, it is of great importance.

Our culture is very sophisticated in providing tools for self-assessment. Some, which will be described later, are formalized tests available at most schools at no cost. Here the emphasis is on what you can do on your own, a sort of a do-it-yourself project in self-discovery. Finding out about yourself is critical in deciding on a major.

Writing as Self-Discovery

Journaling is a popular tool in finding out about oneself. It's not simply keeping a diary. In journaling, people write for many reasons: to establish contact with someone they no longer communicate with, to take their emotional temperature on any given day, or, in this case, to slowly discover what it is that interests them most as far as a major.

As with any new activity, you might not feel as if you are accomplishing anything at first. It takes time. Courses, conferences, and seminars are devoted to learning journaling. People learn how to record their thoughts and feelings to solve a particular problem or to gain insight.

Journaling

Set aside a time every day or even once a week to write what your feelings and thoughts are. Journaling will make you have a conversation with yourself. If you don't take the time to record what you are thinking and feeling, these thoughts and feelings get lost. Joan Didion, the American essayist, said, "I write entirely to find out what I'm thinking, and what I'm looking at, what I see and what it means. What I want and what I fear."

Find a comfortable, quiet place. Have a notebook and pen or pencil. If you prefer to work on a computer screen, that's fine. You may be surprised at what you find yourself writing. After about five weeks of doing this exercise, you will have a clearer picture of what your interests are or at least how you feel about different subjects.

Journal Prompts

The first prompt for the journal is:

Tell me about yourself.

Take time to follow this direction. Use scenes or incidents to describe who you are. Scenes you might include are:

• The first day you went to school

• A really good day

• A funny thing that happened to you

Or, you could start by writing:

My friends say I am . . .

I've changed a lot in the last few years. I used to be . . .

Despite how I seem on the outside, I am . . .

When I wake up in the morning, I look forward to . . .

I hate it when . . .

I'm happiest when . . .

Once upon a time . . .

During the day, I . . .

Time passes quickly for me when . . .

I like people who . . .

I was surprised when I found out . . .

Another way of discovering is to write your name in big block letters. Then tell how your parents chose your name. If you don't know, try to find out.

   Continue with these prompts:

My family likes to . . .

The most important thing I have learned from my mother is . . .

The most important thing I have learned from my father is . . .

When I am not working, I like to . . .

If I could ask one person an important question, I would ask . .

If this person answered the question, he or she would say . . .

An ideal place for me to live would look like . . .

When I go to bed at night, I think about . . .

The classes I enjoy most are those that . . .

Five years from now, I can imagine myself . . .

I've always had a hunch that I would be good at . . .

Despite how I seem on the outside, I am . . .

Journaling involves writing regularly about how you feel and what you imagine. This tool of self-discovery gives you time to really think about yourself. In the rush of a busy world, people forfeit time for self discovery. Taking the time to journal will give you insight into who you are.

Here is what Joe Hirschmugl, a graduate student in English at DePaul University, wrote in finishing the statement "Despite how I seem on the outside, I am . . . ."

"How ya doin'?" The question is simple enough. Everyone asks. For years, I have had trouble finding the words to answer this question. I used to respond, but now realize that this question no longer seems to require an answer. More like a polite greeting, the expected, knee-jerk response is to smile and assure that, like everyone else, I am doing fine, that everything's okay. True or not, I am required to answer so as not to make waves or long faces. Any deviation from the norm would almost seem odd, and I am always wary of putting people in odd positions.

And regardless of whether or not people really listen to my answer, whether they are truly concerned or merely being polite when they ask those three little words, I'm concerned. I am concerned that I cannot tell someone exactly how I am doing, that if I did actually speak my mind or someone actually recognized my deception for what it is, I would somehow be throwing a monkey wrench into a colloquialism better left untouched. Lucky for everyone, though, I am not the type of person who calls undue attention to himself or "tells" people anything they wouldn't want to hear.

In completing the journaling statement, "I'm happiest when . . . ," Jessica Canlas, a recent college graduate who works as an editor for a weekly suburban newspaper, wrote

I'm happiest when I feel as though I'm doing everything I can to maintain and improve myself and my well-being. Whether it be making sure I work out three times a week, making sure I get to church at least a few Sundays a year, or just something as simple as getting the oil in my car changed on time so that my engine doesn't explode, all of this stuff just adds up to me winning the war against one of my most formidable obstacles—laziness. And it's not just about getting up off the couch to change the channel instead of using the remote or making sure I get to work on time. I find myself becoming more and more preoccupied with bettering myself, learning new things, coming to a different understanding of the world around me that some might call more "adultlike"—but I consider it just putting my best effort into living a fulfilling life. None of us wants to end up old and gray, wondering about what could have been or what should have been done—but of course, I believe that that is almost inevitable. At least I hope to be able to console myself with the fact that I tried my best when I was in school, that I tried my best to find a decent job, that I didn't *totally* squander what little money I had—

and, most important, that I didn't push aside my dreams just to make life a little easier or to avoid the disappointment of failure. And that encompasses every aspect of life—physical, spiritual, emotional—just an all-around *whole-feeling* existence.

Read your writing after several weeks and determine what it tells you that you didn't know. On many individual days you will be slightly startled at what you write. Try to step back from the writing and see the you who might be submerged in the outward activity of life. Then ask yourself these questions (or journal them):

Questions to Ask Yourself

1. What activities do I enjoy regularly?_____

2. What kind of people do I enjoy being around? _____

3. What do I value in these activities and these people? _____

4. When do I like myself best? _____

5. What am I good at? _____

6. What activities do I want to try in the future? _____

7. What motivates me to do something new? _____

8. Have I tried anything new lately? _____

9. What am I looking forward to? _____

10. What can I imagine myself doing at a later time in life? _____

11. What stops me from trying new ideas? _____

The Personal Fact Sheet

While the journal promotes knowledge of the inner you, another tool, the Fact Sheet, will help provide the outer you—specifics that may have been long forgotten. Fill out the Fact Sheet, asking relatives besides your parents to provide details when needed. You will be totally surprised at the number of facts and stories you will discover through this project.

Personal Fact Sheet

1. Name: _____ Date: _____

2. Date of birth: _____

3. Place of birth: _____

4. Maiden name of mother: _____

5. Father's name: _____

6. Mother's occupation: _____

7. Father's occupation: _____

8. Parents' place of birth: _____

9. Parents' interests: _____

_____

_____

10. Grandparents' names: _____

_____

_____

11. Grandparents' places of birth: _____

_____

_____

12. Grandparents' occupations: _____

_____

_____

13. Grandparents' interests: _____

_____

_____

14. Occupations of other members of family (sisters, brothers, cousins, aunts, uncles):

_____

_____

15. Interests of other family members: _____

_____

_____

16. Significant neighbors and their occupations: _____

_____

_____

17. Description of a house or apartment your family occupied: _____

_____

_____

18. Description of a car your family owned: _____

_____

_____

19. Organizations your family members joined: _____

_____

_____

20. Description of a typical holiday: _____

_____

_____

21. Weekend activities of your family: _____

_____

_____

22. Pets your family owned and their distinguishing characteristics: _____

_____

_____

23. Events that stand out in the history of your family: _____

_____

_____

24. Accomplishments of members of your family:

_____

_____

Interviewing   Because we interact on a daily basis with friends and family, we take a lot for granted about who they are and who we are in relationship to them. Students interviewing family and friends find that by actually sitting down with a person and taking notes, insights come that are not available in day-to-day living.

Consider asking people in your family to sit with you while you take notes about their lives and the relationships of family members. Unless you do, a rich source of very personal information will be lost.

Questions for a Family Interview

These are some of the questions you might ask, although there are many more:

1. How long has our family been in this country? _____

2. When our ancestors came, how were they employed? _____

3. Why did they settle in this part of the country? _____

4. Have they moved a lot? _____

5. What physical characteristics do many of our family members have? _____

6. How have they been successful? _____

7. What are some of the best traits of our family members? _____

8. Have I met all our relatives?_____

9. If not, where are they and what are they doing? _____

10. Do you mind if I write to them? _____

11. What is a good way to find their addresses? _____

12. Why don't we have contact with them? _____

13. Do all our relatives practice the same religion? _____

14. What illnesses seem to run in the family? _____

15. What are the values of our family? What do we treasure? _____

16. Have people in our family gone to college? _____

17. What did they major in? _____

18. What did they do career-wise after college? _____

19. Can you think of any career regrets in our family? _____

20. Have our relatives had many different jobs? _____

21. Do you know why they decided to change jobs? _____

22. How did those decisions work out for them? _____

23. Do you have any good advice to pass on? _____

Grandparents and great-grandparents are excellent sources of information on family traits and history. Parents may be less help in finding out what has gone before because they may still be fairly young. Aunts, uncles, and cousins add special information because their memories will be different from your immediate family's.

After you have interviewed family members, a picture of your family will emerge. Perhaps many people in your family have owned their own businesses, some successfully, others not. Some families have many members in the sciences. Others have a tradition of finishing high school and then working with their hands. Knowing what has gone before is knowing what influences you and perhaps limits you in your choice of major. If no one in your family, for instance, has gone to college, much less considered majoring in history, you may feel uncomfortable and cave in to familial pressure to choose a "practical" major. Parents without college experience may resent your absence from family affairs because you have to study. "She's always in the room with the books," they may complain, or they may not understand when it takes you five years to finish school. In these cases, the student might be a catalyst for change. If one member goes to college, others in the family might consider it as well.

The Minibiography

Writing a minibiography, five or ten pages, will help you discover new aspects of yourself. Start with a page of all the facts you can discover. Some are easy, gathered from your fact sheet. Other facts to include are described in the following paragraphs.

- Where were you born? At home? In a hospital? What number child were you? Firstborn? Middle? Number six? Your birth certificate supplies much of this information. It's surprising how many people have never seen their birth certificates. Were you adopted? If you were, the birth certificate your parents have may not be the original. Theirs may merely certify that they are your legal parents, not your biological parents.
- What time of day were you born? What was going on in the world?
- What were your parents' occupations at the time of your birth? Did your mother return to work after

you were born? Who took care of you? What kind of community were you raised in? Did you live in an urban setting, in the suburbs, on a farm, on a reservation?

- List all the schools you attended. With the average American selling his or her home every seven years, most children transfer schools many times. Which school was your favorite? Why?
- Were you educated in public, parochial, or private schools? Were you in the United States the whole time, or did you study overseas also?
- During your growing-up years, how did you spend your spare time? Was yours a home where the television was usually on or off? Was there a park nearby where children gathered? Did you spend time learning skills such as karate, piano, gymnastics, basketball, computers?
- Did you come from a family that encouraged new experiences or that felt more comfortable with the tried and true? Write examples.
- What were your brothers, sisters, cousins interested in?
- How did your parents spend their spare time? How often did other people visit your home?
- What has been your work experience? Write about how you happened to get each of the jobs. Did you have choices?
- What has been your community involvement? Does your family take part in community or church activities on a regular basis?

It might take you some time to get these facts together. From them, a distinct picture of your life to date will become clearer.

Now add a couple of imaginary paragraphs to the minibiography. Mention your college major and what you were involved in the first few years after college. An imaginary scenario might be:

> *Your name* chose anthropology as her/his major in college and after graduation worked for a nonprofit agency in Appalachia, providing social services. After two years he/she decided he/she wanted to become a doctor and took postbaccalaureate classes in the sciences to prepare for the MCAT (admissions tests for medical school). Now *your name* is studying medicine at *make up name of school.*

Family Traits

Many students say they are different from their families. Others say adamantly that they don't want to be like members of their family. However, most people are like their families, even though they don't want to admit it. They vote for the same political party their family has voted for, they buy the same type of products they had in their home, they have or don't have pets, depending on the home they were raised in. When young, you may appear to be the opposite of your family, but as the years go by, the chances are great that you will be similar to them. If many members of your family go into pharmacy, you need to realize that you are not obligated to follow the familial path. Just knowing what the composite of your family is will help you to know more about your choices.

Tonya's Story. Tonya is the first person in her family to go to college, and her aunts always tell her she is a fool. They are making good money owning their own beauty shops and think that Tonya is wasting her time majoring in communications.

"What good is that going to do you?" they ask her at every family gathering. Her mother tells them to leave her alone but it leaves Tonya anxious about whether she's made the right choice, her future ability to pay off her student loans, and wondering if they're right about her putting on airs just because she's in college. She doesn't know any of the answers yet, but this family does not value a liberal arts degree. Their value system is the practical, the only one they have ever known.

The Family Traits Tree. Most of us have filled out a family tree in school. Usually, they merely tell the names, birthdates, and death dates of our relatives. People interested in genetic diseases are now adding health histories to these trees. What we are going to add is family traits. Your cousin Ida's ability to braid hair beautifully and carefully, for instance, might indicate fine motor skills as well as the ability to focus and concentrate. Your Uncle Robert's ability to play a musical instrument without reading notes is noteworthy and unusual. Many times people seem more similar to an aunt or uncle than to one of their parents. So design your own family traits tree here, indicating the main traits or skills your family has demonstrated. Try to talk to the older people in your family to find out about relatives who have died.

Family Traits Tree

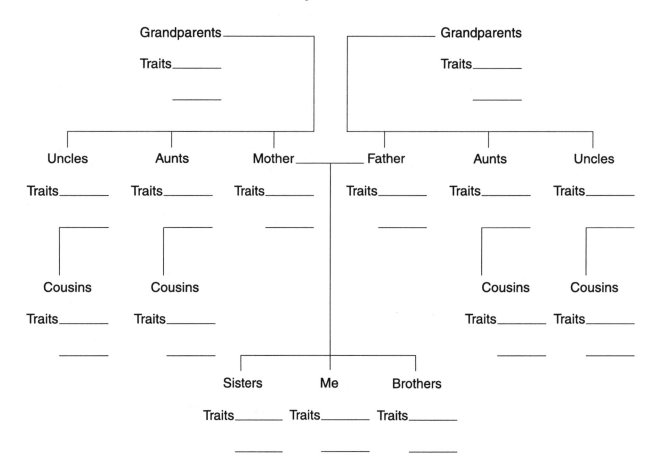

Testing   Wouldn't this all be easier if you could just take a battery of tests to tell you what you are good at and what you want to do? It would be exquisitely easy, but research on even the most widely used tests for aptitude and interests indicates that the tests are not entirely accurate. They are a tool and provide a basis for decisions, but they do not reflect your intuitive sense of what is the best path for you.

However, many tests are available to you free, either at the high school guidance office or in the career counseling office of the college you attend or are thinking of attending.

Myers-Briggs Type Indicator (MBTI)*   The Myers-Briggs, as it is popularly called, is a well-known test. Designed by two American women, Katharine Briggs and her daughter, Isabel Briggs Myers, the MBTI tests and describes personalities. Using four personality preference scales and sixteen distinct personality types,

*Both these names are registered trademarks of Consulting Psychologists Press.

the test was designed to discover how personality fits into theworld of school and work. The women based their work on the discoveries of Carl Jung, an eclectic psychoanalyst and disciple of Sigmund Freud. The test may be used as a tool to help you discover your motivations and preferences. Try to take it twice within a few months to see if you are consistent in your choices.

The MBTI personality assessment deals with four aspects of personality:

1. How you interact with the world and where you direct your energy: Extravert, Introvert (E, I)

2. How you normally notice information: Sensing, Intuition (S, I)

3. How you make decisions: Thinking, Feeling (T, F)

4. How you interact with the environment: Judging, Perceiving (J, P)

After you have been tested by someone authorized to administer the test, you will have a four-letter label indicating your personality type. A counselor may use this as a basis for reviewing what career options might be most appropriate.

Some college counseling centers offer group sessions to people who have taken the test to analyze the results and hear what the individual sets of letters mean. A book on the subject, *Do What You Are,* by Paul D. Tieger and Barbara Barron-Tieger, offers examples of personality-career correlation.

Strong Interest Inventory (SII)

The Strong Interest Inventory is the most widely used test for vocational assessment. Administered at both high schools and colleges, and for adults, it was first published in 1927 by E. K. Strong and was rewritten most recently in 1994. Consisting of 317 items, the test asks the taker to evaluate his or her preferences for different occupations on a Like/Indifferent/Dislike matrix. Your counselor at school can explain the test and help you evaluate the results.

Other Tests

Besides the Strong Interest Inventory (SII) and the Myers-Briggs Type Indicator (MBTI), there are many other vocational interest tests used at school counseling offices.

Whether you feel the results of the tests are reliable or not, they at least provide you with the vocabulary used in vocational assessment and give you the opportunity to talk with a counselor about your interests. After taking the tests you will need a qualified person to interpret the results and counsel you on their implications for your future.

Interviewing People You Know Outside the Family

Much informal interviewing goes on at block parties, between golfers and their caddies, between babysitters and the people they work for. These are ideal opportunities for young people to find information on college majors and careers. Working in a dental office, on a tree farm, or at the library provides countless opportunities for meeting people outside the family whom you can interview. These exchanges are like information interviews on a professional level, which will be detailed in Chapter 3, but they are much less formal and less intimidating.

Setting Up the Informal Interview

First, you must ask the person if he or she would be willing to sit down with you and talk about what he or she does. This has to be time that the person has volunteered, not time when you are being paid.

After you have expressed a sincere interest in finding out what this person does, set up a time when you can talk, uninterrupted. For most young people, this is a difficult request to make, but the reward will be very useful information.

You don't have to take notes. In fact, notetaking may interfere with the free flow of conversation. Some of the questions you might ask are:

1. What actually do you do at your job?
2. How long have you been there?
3. What was your college major?
4. How did you decide on that major?
5. Are you satisfied with the major you chose?
6. How does it help you on the job?
7. How does it help you in other areas of your life?
8. What's the best part of your work?
9. What's the worst part of your work?
10. How is your field changing?

11. If you have kids do you think they'll go into your field?

12. What kind of people are attracted to your field?

13. What kind of hours do you work?

14. Does your job require travel?

15. What additional schooling did you need to improve your skills?

16. What job advice would you give a young person today?

Students are surprised at how willing adults are to share their years of wisdom and what useful information and impressions they get from merely setting aside time to talk with people they know. After the interview students see these people in a new light, not merely as a weekend golfer, a mother of two toddlers, or the friendly veterinarian. You will gain insight and knowledge from these people if only you take the time to ask them questions.

Your Skills

Many of the skills you have now will be sharpened as you move through college. It's helpful to know what you started with. Students are often reluctant to admit they know anything about their own skills. The skills worksheet on pages 42–43 will help you identify your skills.

Skills Worksheet

What am I good at?_____

_____

_____

_____

What examples do I have of this?_____

_____

_____

_____

Have I been encouraged to develop what I am good at? _____

By whom?_____

_____

What do I think I might be good at? _____

_____

_____

How can I find out? _____

_____

_____

Who can help me learn more about this? _____

_____

_____

What am I interested in? _____

_____

_____

Have I had much exposure to this subject? _____ _____

How can I find out more about it? _____

_____

_____

My friends would describe my skills as _____

_____

_____

_____

My family would describe my skills as _____

_____

_____

_____

In high school, I got good grades in _____

_____

My grades didn't reflect my skills because _____

_____

_____

_____

A Student Profile   Anthony, a senior at a public high school on the West Coast, said this about his skills:

> Since I was about eight my mother has let me cook with her. By the time I was fourteen I was starting to be a better cook than she was. I'd look at recipes and see how they could be improved. I have a big appetite, like everyone else in our family. They are all happy when I cook. Along the way, I started growing herbs

because fresh always tastes better than a jar from the store. But then, I started getting really interested in computers too, so now I only cook when I am starved. My father lent me the money to start my own computer company when I was sixteen. I provided my clients with access to the Internet. Right now I'm helping a restaurant owner make his operation more efficient with the help of computers. I know a lot about computers and a lot about food. I don't do well with subjects like English and history that require a lot of reading. I don't get good grades at school because I have so many outside interests. I'm looking at colleges that have strong computer majors and business courses. I guess one of my skills is curiosity and another is I can stay with something until it works.

Your Skill Profile

Look at the following list of skills and circle the ones you already have. Next, go through the list again and put an X next to the skills you want to develop.

Logic

Attention to detail

Drawing

Mechanical

Creative

Social

Research

Planning

Language

Discussion

Design

Communication

Writing

Reading

Performance

Problem solving

Daily living

Preparation

Decision making

Loyalty

Athletic

Honesty

Confidence

List three skills from the list or others that you would like to develop:

1. _____

2. _____

3. _____

How are you going to develop these skills? Where can you get help developing these skills?

The I'm-Going-to-Do-It Principle

Most of skill development is the I'm-going-to-do-it principle. Once you have decided that a particular skill is desirable, you can start developing your aptitude for it. What happens if you find you have little or no aptitude for this skill? You do what you can and move on to the next one you want to develop.

One Student's Solution to Performance Anxiety. When Dontrey started playing the clarinet in junior high school she would become paralyzed with fear whenever her school had a band night. The band director was a kind person but he needed everyone there to play. Even at this young age, she knew she had to overcome her fear of performing. The price she was paying was too high: extreme anxiety with upset stomach before the performance, exhaustion afterwards and zombie-like feelings the next day.

When auditions were held in high school for the play *To Kill a Mockingbird*, she tried out for one of the minor parts, got it, memorized her lines perfectly, and forced herself to perform. Building on her initial triumph over stage fright, she got a part in *Major Barbara* junior year, and in senior year she played the part of the nun in *The Prime of Miss Jean Brodie*.

She did not major in drama or theater in college but chose biology. The performance skills she had worked so hard to develop served her well senior year as a teaching assistant. She led a class of twenty students after the large weekly 400-person lecture with a professor.

Your Values

All people have personal values based on their families, their communities, their religious or non-religious affiliations, their experiences. Values are an important part of deciding what major you will pursue. The major must reflect your values. If it doesn't, your life will be in conflict. The stereotypical case is the student who probably should be a liberal arts major, but decides to major in business, hearing that people who major in business make more money. Answer the following questions in your journaling notebook to help define what your values are.

1. How would you describe a successful person? Based on this description, how successful have you been so far?

2. If supporting yourself, and in the future, a family, was not a concern, how would you spend your time?

3. If you were offered a million dollars to give up one of your friendships, what would you do?

4. What do you hope to achieve in the years ahead?

5. Is there anything you would like to change about yourself?

6. Have there been experiences or people who have changed or influenced your way of thinking?

7. What do you value in other people?

8. What do you value about yourself?

9. What does your community value? (Hard work? Country club membership? Saving money? Supporting those in need? Fair rules for everyone? Universal education? etc.)

10. What does your family value? (Getting ahead? Looking good? Frugality? Social life? etc.)

11. Do you admire your parents' values?

The Tripod of Skills, Values, and Interests

Your choice of major sits on top of a tripod. Skills, values, and interests form the legs. Each part must be represented or the major will topple over. Try to think carefully about each of the three parts.

Sylvia Has Skill But No Interest

Sylvia is a high school math whiz. Teachers tell her she could be an astronaut. She knows math is important in society, and she wants to work on something important in life. The problem is, she doesn't want to study math any further. Her intuition tells her there's something else for her. "When I get to college this fall, I'm just going to look around and see what's available. I'm going to bug professors in different departments until I find what I need to know about other majors. Is there a major in therapeutic gardening?" She also will have the advantage of taking a variety of different subjects her freshman and sophomore year.

The Total Picture

Take a good, long look at the composite you have formed through these exercises and ask yourself:

1. How am I like members of my family?
2. How am I not like them?
3. What skills do I have?
4. What do I value?
5. What am I interested in?
6. What motivates me?
7. Who am I?

Guiding Lights

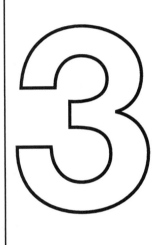

Even the Lone Ranger had Tonto. Rarely do people accomplish much without the help of others. As humans we were designed to live in supportive communities where others encourage us when we stumble along our path. "I'll get by with a little help from my friends" holds true.

When the human tribe was smaller and simpler, perhaps it was easier to figure out what you were supposed to do with your life. In prehistoric times your choices were limited. First of all, you wouldn't be doing it for very long—life expectancy was much shorter than today's 70s. The tribe might have determined that you would be a good hunter, while others did the fishing. Or you became the leader of the gatherers. You might have been in charge of keeping the fires burning. Or healing. The tribe knew who was good at what.

Today, the tribe is much larger and, as a result, has established complex systems for survival. The tribe doesn't know what you're capable of. First you choose what you would like to do, the colleges determine if you have the skill, then you compete in the workforce for the job that fits best with your skills and temperament.

College is the time when you part from your parents and become independent and capable of making your own decisions. Even people who live at home during college are separating from their parents, learning to think independently in their studies and to be responsible for their own schedules and deadlines.

To make sense of this huge system, you need help. Getting the courage to ask for help is sometimes the hardest part. No one can know everything about the best major for you. Hunches, guesses, and gossip may lead you down the wrong path. You need up-to-date facts from people who deal with the subject every day. You also need advice from people who are actually in the major field you are considering.

So take advantage of any light that can be thrown on the subject—a searchlight, a headlight, a beacon, starlight, a votive candle. They will light the way to your major.

Searchlights: High School College Counselors

Some students are afraid to even go to the door of the high school college counselor's office. Planning for college admittedly is a big step. But what do you have to lose? If no one went in, this counselor wouldn't have a job. So you're doing him or her a favor by going, think of it that way.

You may go to a small high school where not many people go on to college. Your school may be suburban and very college prep, with a college counseling office designed like a war room with maps, dates of engagement, assaults on campuses, and so on. Whatever the situation, counselors are the experts. They study, hear, ask about, and assimilate a great deal of information about colleges.

However, many are reluctant to advise on long plans incorporating college majors and careers. "At our counselor conferences some say to me 'I don't need to talk to the seniors about careers because 98 percent of ours go on to college'," related one counselor, who starts students thinking about majors their freshman year in high school.

Most college counseling offices are crammed with promotional materials from many colleges, and directories giving the addresses of lesser-known colleges that might not recruit at your school. Many offices are equipped with computers to search for information on the schools in which you have an interest.

Be patient with the college counseling staff. They see hundreds of students in a month. The first time you visit may not be perfect. They don't know you yet. Go back again, a second and third time. If they have seen your face once, they will be more receptive next time. It's an old cliché, but the squeaky wheel generally gets the grease. Eventually, as the counseling staff get to know you and have a sense of what you need, they will have a personal interest in your success.

Before the Appointment

One way to get prepared for talking with the counselor is to compose a sheet of basic information about yourself. The office may have a profile of you on file, but it may not include the illuminating specifics that make you unique.

Here are facts you might list:

Name

Year of school

Favorite subjects so far

Extracurricular activities

Clubs

Outside interests

Foreign languages

Musical instrument

Special talents

Subjects you want to explore

Parents' occupations

Number of siblings and what they are doing

Career ideas

College geographic desirability

Anticipated financial support or nonsupport for college

Questions for the Counselor

Next, make a list of questions you have for the counselor. It's normal to be totally unsure about what you're doing at this stage of the game. The counselors are trained to help you find answers to your questions. The process doesn't seem as complicated to students with older brothers or sisters at college. If you ask older siblings, they might give good advice.

Some high schools require freshmen to accumulate information on themselves in a folder for college counseling. As new information about the students is available, such as the results of interest inventory tests, the folder grows. During the four years of high school, it begins to resemble an FBI file. When you look at your folder you will see how your thinking about college and majors has evolved during the four years.

Saying "duh" with a shrug of the shoulders is not a focused way to start a meeting with a counselor. Pre-work is necessary. Pick three even vaguely interesting majors. Prepare a list of about ten schools. Then the counselor will have a basis for conversation. Most students choose schools that are close to where they live geographically. They don't want to travel thousands of miles to get home, plus at the state schools they want to take advantage of the lower tuition schedule for state residents.

Reading Lights: College Guidebooks and Rankings

Especially if your school is understaffed in the college counseling area, you will need to do a lot of the detective work on your own. Even though your schedule is already crammed with school work and outside interests and activities, you need to find the time to review not only what colleges you are interested in, but whether they offer the subjects that seem to interest you now.

Bookstores and libraries are filled with books that list statistics and information on colleges. Among those available are:

> *Barron's Profiles of American Colleges*
>
> *Cass & Birnbaum's Guide to American Colleges*
>
> *Colleges That Change Lives,* Loren Pope (Penquin)
>
> *Peterson's Four-Year Colleges*
>
> *The College Handbook,* The College Board
>
> *The Complete Book of College,* The Princeton Review
>
> *The Fiske Guide to Colleges*
>
> *The Insider's Guide to the Colleges,* compiled and edited by the staff of the Yale Daily News

Some of the guides are published separately by geographical region, and others offer information for specific groups, such as minorities and art majors.

Statistical information on a college does not present the total picture. These numbers cannot tell you that a department in a college is going to be eliminated next year. You may be adverse to attending a school that has a strong Greek system or does not support the female students as much as the males. This type of information is found through word of mouth or the Internet, or by reading a book such as *The Insider's Guide to the Colleges*, compiled and edited by the staff of the Yale Daily News. Once you mention interest in a major to friends and family, you give them the opportunity to think of other contacts who can supply additional information to you.

Many students make the mistake of choosing a college based on its name recognition rather than its expertise in a particular field. Looking at the listings in *U.S. News & World Report*'s annual "America's Best Colleges," for instance, you may think that the top-rated schools offer every major you are interested in and that the schools excel in all these fields. You may have an interest in gerontology, the study of aging, but a small liberal arts college is not likely to offer a major in this field. The rankings get a great deal of publicity, but you need to research the individual departments you are considering as a major. Check for books in the college counseling office that actually rank departments within the schools you are considering.

In 1996 the press reported complaints that some colleges were providing one set of data to financial rating agencies and another to those writing guidebooks, publishing rankings, or providing college information for books and software. Now, a standardized questionnaire has been written for the more than forty kinds of data commonly requested by magazines such as *U.S. News & World Report* and *Money* magazine. This standardized form was designed to clear up problems of the past, such as including foreign students in averaging SAT scores or inflating the size of a college faculty by adding part-time instructors. Even with the new form, the magazines do not have the resources to cross check the information provided by the colleges. Then there is the problem of data entry errors. In 1996, *U.S. News & World Report* ranked American University 121st, when its actual ranking was 105th, eleven slots higher than the school ranked in 1995. Errors happen.

The guidebooks are excellent resources for those who take time to read and compare what different schools have to offer. Each guidebook offers slightly different approaches to looking at a school. Reading more than one will provide insight into the range of majors offered, the most popular majors because of the reputation of that discipline at the school, and the amount of academic pressure. Some guidebooks spell out the academic pressure and others merely cite the mean SAT and ACT scores, giving an indication of how tough or easy it is going to be to complete a program successfully.

Starlights: Your Hunches and Dreams

At this stage in your life it is extremely difficult to say with certainty what you want to major in and subsequently use in a career. You are just "channel surfing."

"I think we should celebrate the undecided student," said Sue Biemeret, the guidance counselor at the Adlai E. Stevenson High School, a large, rapidly expanding high school in suburban Chicago. "Careers constantly change. I don't think you can know at eighteen what to major in. That's why so many schools have a core curriculum of liberal arts courses. Students are required to study a variety of subjects in order to become intellectually well-rounded and to be exposed to a wide variety of subjects. Colleges do not expect students to have their futures all planned out freshman year.

"We try to put the emphasis more on learning the skill of decision making. This means they should be examining their academic strengths and weaknesses. They should think about what classes they liked most and liked least. They should be examining their values," she said.

The Stevenson "Countdown to College" booklet for students has this advice:

> One final word of caution regarding majors. *Careers* are not always identical to *majors*. Many successful people in education, industry, and the health professions did not major in their career area as a college student. Your career is the end result of three factors: your college major, your work experiences, and your changing interests. Since the average American changes careers six times in his/her lifetime, a college major often is not the sole requirement for a career. We encourage you to study a field in which you're most interested. You'll get the most out of college if you put the most into it.

Mrs. Biemeret has been counseling students on college choices for many years. Her experience has shown her the importance of students making their own choices and not relying on their parents to do the decision making for them.

Counselors not only teach how to "talk the talk" using the vocabulary and process of college admissions but also, and more importantly, should explore your dreams for the future and your hunches about what's right for you. The data on colleges can be overwhelming at times but the focus of exploring your personal intuitive sense of your own direction should not get lost in the blizzard of information in the counselor's office.

Headlights: Parents

The next people to ask about majors are your parents. "It's amazing how many kids have no idea what their parents do for a living," said Sue Wendt, the guidance counselor at Lyons Township High School in LaGrange, Illinois. "'My dad has some high-pressure job and comes home crabby at night,' is typical of what students will say when I ask about their parents' jobs," she added.

The goal is not to have parents making the decision, but for parents to aid and support you in your decision. At the minimum, they supply another pair of eyes and ears to assess the information you are gathering. This is the ideal situation.

However, some parents impede the process. At one end of the spectrum are the parents who don't want to become involved at all, for a number of their own reasons. At the other end are parents who are too involved, potentially inhibiting your efforts in decision making. Many parents have not gone to college, and for those who have, the college experience is completely different today with coed dorms, rollerblading to class, and condoms in vending machines.

A Technical Education

Sometimes it takes awhile for parents to accept the fact that a four-year institution is not the best way for everyone to get an education. Technical schools and junior colleges often offer the best option for students who do not want to be immersed in the collegiate experience. The technical schools offer training toward a specific skill and usually cost less than traditional colleges. Junior colleges introduce students to academic life and offer a chance to earn an associate's degree.

"Our students are pragmatic and not looking for a wealth of personal development," said John Petrik, the dean of placement and student affairs at DeVry Institutes, a publicly owned company that offers technology-based education at 13 campuses in North America. The campuses are devoid of cultural activities. Students make pit stops to take classes and are out of there. The DeVry students finish college degrees quickly because of year-round classes. The focus of the schools is applied education, with bachelor's degrees offered in accounting, business operations, computer information systems, electronics engineering technology, telecommunications management, and technical management. Most finish their degrees within three years at a cost of under $30,000. DeVry says it places more than 91 percent of its graduates in jobs within six months of graduation.

Time Out

Parents might be fearful, also, of their daughter or son taking time off before going to school. When a student is unenthusiastic about the prospect of going to college, however, time out may be the best option. The book *Taking Time Off*, by Colin Hall and Ron Lieber, offers thirty-three first-person accounts from people who have taken an extended break before or during college. To find resources for planning time off, ask your high school college counselor or the advising office of your college. Consulting firms, such as Interim in Boston, are in the business of providing information on how to plan time off.

Another group of parents is adamant that their children know "what he or she is going to do with this degree" before they even start. This is where the campus visits are helpful. Going with a guide, an upperclassperson, and other families around a campus serves to educate everyone about the college process. Parents will see that most students have only a vague notion of what they want to major in. Students not knowing is more common than the parents suspected.

Whatever category your parents fall in, it is best to begin talking with them about your considerations. You are being educated about schools and they will be, too. Gathering information and sharing it is the first step.

Enlightenment: Career Days and Nights

College students get a chance to interview companies for jobs at career days. High school students hear working professionals talk about their jobs at career nights. There's a lot to be learned at these events. Even if your school does not sponsor these events, it is still possible for you to attend a career day or night. The schools planning these events put announcements in the newspapers and on radio. Call and see if all students are welcome.

Dress-for-success attire fills the gymnasium at a career day. No applicant comes in wearing a baseball hat backwards. Toting briefcases filled with resumes, the seniors repeatedly shake hands with interviewers as they go from table to table to hear about individual companies and potential jobs. Long before you are scheduled to work in the outside world you should attend a career day. Talking with human resource personnel gives you an opportunity to hear the language, get used to the dynamics, and see which majors companies are hiring.

The recruiters appreciate the students who come up to the table, shake hands confidently, and say what they are interested in doing. If you don't know yet, you can mention the areas that interest you. You will be amazed at the information these people have to share. They know trends, salaries, educational requirements, the culture of the organization they represent, and many other aspects of working.

Usually the event organizers have set up a space at one end for company representatives to interview prospective employees. They can quickly tell if the student is the kind of person and has the skills the company is looking for. Or they may ask the student to come to an interview at the site of the company.

The energy at a job fair or a career day is high because students are hopeful that they have made a good connection and may get hired. These events are also exhausting, with so many possibilities and only a short time to pursue each one.

Even if you are a long way from graduation, career days are useful for you to attend. Recruiters have spare time and are eager to be busy and talking to students. They understand that some students are on fishing expeditions and not yet serious about job hunting. Use this time to gain information for yourself about career paths.

Beacons: Information Interviews

One of the best ways to find out about a potential career is to ask a working professional for an interview. These specifically are called "information interviews," and working professionals are familiar with the term.

Normally, the word "interview" scares students, but in this form, the student or potential job seeker goes out and conducts the interview with working professionals who are willing to give a half an hour or more of their time to talk about what they actually do at work and what they see as the future for their industry.

It's hard, perhaps, to imagine why a working person would take time out of his or her busy day to be interviewed by a student. Still, many do agree. Some have signed up with the alumni office of their colleges as willing volunteers for such an interview. Others are flattered when a young person calls. Many people who are in responsible positions feel they have an obligation to continue educating people about their professions.

Sources of information interviews can be found in many places, even the bus ride on the way home. You may strike up a conversation with the person next to you and he or she may give you a business card. Great! Chance meetings provide many networking opportunities in the future.

It is never too early to start conducting information interviews. The main skill involved is initiative. You must decide to call people and ask them for time.

A low-stress information interview, such as one with a neighbor or a friend at his or her place of work, is a good way to start. Besides people you know, make a list of ten people or organizations you might call. You also can get names of companies or organizations from the library.

The human resources (HR) department is where all records of employees are kept. Movies and action videos generally don't star the people in HR, but these hardworking people placers can be extremely good sources of information about the people you need to see.

Make up your list with phone numbers and enough space after each person's name or after each organization for notes.

This has to be regarded as a skill-building campaign. People who have never had an interview or conducted an interview don't do as well as those who have become familiar with the process. The earlier you start the better.

The first call is the most stressful. After that you will become a pro. Your most important tool is the phone. You may be nervous, but increasingly you will get better. You might have a script in front of you, like the ones you've heard from telemarketers. This script can be used whether you are calling the human resources department of a company or are calling the person you want to interview directly. Remember, you may have to make eight phone calls before you get a nibble. Don't take any of the responses personally. People are rushed sometimes, don't understand the request, or are not familiar with the process. You will get better the more times you do this project.

Script for Information Interview Request

Hello, Mr. or Ms. _____ My name is _____

I am a _____(name year and school).

I got your name from _____and I'm calling to find
information on the field of _____
(the person's career field). I am not looking for a job, but I would greatly appreciate hearing about your
work experience in the field of _____(name
the area this person works in). I would appreciate 20 minutes of your time and am available as early
as 7:30 any morning.

(This latter statement will really impress the person. Most busy people start work early and if you meet with one then you will not be interrupted by phone calls and other problems. Plus, suggesting this early time means you are really a go-getter.)

The person you are calling might readily agree or might put you off because he or she is in the middle of an extremely hectic project. If the person can do it, fine. If not, politely thank him or her and move on to the next person on your list. It might take eight calls before you get a person to accept, but then again, it may take only one call.

Once you have set the time, date, and place for the interview, start doing your homework. You must have a list of prepared questions. People see top television interviewers such as Katie Couric or Matt Lauer, who make it seem effortless. Both these interviewers are very hard workers who also have researchers to look up information and help prepare their lists of questions. They can't possibly know all the details of the lives of the many people they interview. Who can remember off the top of his or her head how old Madonna is or if John Travolta earned an Oscar for *Saturday Night Fever*? They have to do research and be prepared, just as you will.

A list of ten questions, written out, will be sufficient. Here are typical questions asked in these interviews, although there are many more that might be better for you:

How did you get this job?

How long have you been with this company?

What kind of training or education is necessary for your position?

What is the culture of the company? (Many professionals don't think about this question until an interviewer asks it. If your person needs a prompt, ask what the values of the company are and how those are demonstrated on a day-to-day basis.)

What do you actually do each day?

What hours do you work? Do you work evenings, weekends, or overtime? Are you compensated for extra time?

Do you have any travel in your job?

Are you part of a team?

If so, what is your role?

What is the best part of your job?

What is the worst part of your job?

How is your time divided between working with people, data, technology?

What skills and talents are necessary in getting your job done?

How much variety is there in your work?

Do you get enough input from supervisors?

How much stress are you under?

How does the company motivate you?

How much contact do you have with people outside the company?

Are there any advantages or disadvantages in being a woman or a man in this job?

How is your industry changing?

Is there much social life with other employees?

What is the entry-level salary in this field?

If you had it to do all over again, would you major in anything different in college?

Is it important in your field to continue to take courses?

What do young people need to know about the world of work?

Does your company employ people with a variety of majors?

Is a master's degree required for people in your field?

Can you recommend other people who would talk to me about this field?

You can scribble the person's answers in a notebook, or, with permission, use a tape recorder. Tape recorders make many people very nervous and hesitant to say what they are really thinking in response to your questions. Or you may just sit and listen attentively.

Besides preparing questions, a few other plans need to be made before the interview. Know exactly how to get there and how long it will take. In large metropolitan areas today, travel time is extended by weather conditions, road construction, and accidents, so give yourself plenty of time. Plan on arriving twenty minutes early. Bring something to read so that you will not get restless.

Interview Etiquette   Dress neatly. When the person comes to the waiting room to meet you, stand up, shake hands, and say "Thank you for your time," and refresh the person's memory about who you are and where you go to school. In this extremely busy world people appreciate review. Even though you may be nervous about conducting this interview, the person being interviewed may be nervous also. Even though you may feel as if you are just a lowly student who has been granted this enormous favor, the person being interviewed may feel a bit anxious about having to answer all these direct questions. Most people aren't interviewed every day and are as self-conscious as you about their grammar, their answers, their diction. A good way to make everyone feel at ease is to have your questions prepared, tell the person how many you have, and tell him or her at various points how far along you are in your questions. "My sixth question out of the ten I have prepared is . . . ."

At the end of the appointment tell the individual how much you have appreciated the time and the information. Be specific, say what impressed you or what you did not know before the interview that you learned. Manage your interview to last twenty minutes. You may be encouraged to stay longer, but do not stay beyond thirty minutes. These are busy people.

Respecting other people's time is a sign of maturity. Time is scarce and everyone appreciates consideration of this valuable resource. If there is a secretary or receptionist who helped to set up the interview, remember to thank this person also on your way out.

Some obvious points:

1. Don't chew gum.
2. Don't light up a cigarette.
3. Don't touch anything on the person's desk.
4. Offer to excuse yourself if a phone call comes in.

If, for some reason, you get to the interview and it has been cancelled, politely ask for a rescheduling. People get called out of town, they get sick, their kids get sick, there can be many reasons for a cancelled interview. It happens. Don't let this temporary setback stand in your way. Set the time for another interview. Or, ask if there is anyone else you could interview, as long as you are already there. Some people are willing to substitute for missing colleagues.

Another problem is when the interviewer repeatedly takes phone calls during the interview. Ask each time if you should leave but don't lose your train of thought. Keep returning to your questions.

Write a thank-you note immediately upon returning home. It might read:

Dear (Mr. or Ms., not Miss or Mrs.)

The time you spent with me on (name of day) was extremely helpful in broadening my knowledge of the field of (name area). I was impressed with (name something the person told you, such as the volume of sales of his or her company, the number of hours required each week at work, the variety of tasks required each day).

I hope you continue to enjoy deserved success at (name of organization).

Yours truly,
Signature
Your name typed
Phone number
Date

These notes should be typed, but if typing is going to delay the note being written, write it out on plain note paper. The main point is to get it done. There are two advantages to doing it right away:

1. You won't have the nagging feeling that you should be writing a thank-you note.

2. The person will see your name once again and is apt to remember you as a polite, well-organized individual should your paths ever cross in the future, particularly after college when you will be using all the contacts you have ever made to get a job.

For your own benefit, type or write the results of the interview. Your initial impressions of what the person said might seem dramatically different six months later when you are reviewing all your interviews.

Your Reaction to the Interview

Suppose you interviewed an accountant because that's the field you are considering majoring in. You may have three different reactions to the interview:

1. You may be excited because the job seems even more desirable than you had imagined; you hadn't realized before the interview that accountants today have so much interaction with clients.

2. You may feel dazed because you realize that there's a lot more you need to find out about what different fields of accounting involve before you decide to major in this field.

3. You may feel discouraged because you didn't like what you heard and can't imagine yourself working in this field, based on what this person told you.

Whether the answer is 1, 2, or 3 in the preceding list, you must conduct more information interviews. Conclusions cannot be reached on the basis of just one interview. If the answer is:

1. You need to check to make sure the person you interviewed wasn't painting too rosy a picture of the field of accounting. He or she might have unconsciously been trying to lure you to this field and minimizing the negatives.

2. You are dazed because the enormity of the field has hit you. Better that it hit you now rather than after graduation. The shock of graduating and then finding out about your prospects is overwhelming.

3. It's time to look at other fields in addition to the one

you've been considering. Consider yourself very fortunate at this stage because many people don't realize until the first month on the job what they have actually gotten themselves into. And this includes lawyers, doctors, people with doctorates in every field. Without prior knowledge, many are stunned to discover the reality of the work situation that they couldn't know merely by going to school.

Information interviews are more crucial today than ever before because each field is changing so quickly, and every job is enormously specialized. Different areas of the country offer different types of jobs in the same field. Only by going out as your own career reporter can you find what you need to know. And high school is not too early to begin.

Take Advantage of Interviews

Most people you ask to be interviewed will be very receptive to you. It gives them a chance to give back to a young person and time to reflect on what they are actually doing at work.

Take what every person says to you with suspended belief, or a grain of salt, as grandma used to say. You only are getting the view of one person in one field, and there are thousands of others. You may interview this person on a really good day, or on a really bad day. Most people are very conscientious about conveying information to suggestible young people, but you have to remain objective yourself. If you interview five accountants and they all tell you that they have lots of client contact in their work, then you can be reasonably sure that this is a main part of being an accountant today. Or if five pharmacists say they feel they are serving an important need by providing important drug information and a friendly face when people aren't feeling well, you can be confident that this represents the field.

The danger is merely interviewing one person and drawing conclusions that may or may not be correct. If you were a newspaper reporter, you would have to check out any statements made to you by people you interviewed. Consider your source's comments an open door to a room. Go in and look at the room's contents more closely. Give yourself enough time to look at the room—don't scurry around and exit before you've noticed all the furniture, the carpeting, the lighting, the space. How does the room look? How does it feel when you're in it?

Many seniors in college conduct information interviews before they enter the job market. Occasionally they get a job offer as a result of the interview even though this is not what was planned. It's considered bad form to ask about the possibility of employment during an information interview. Several months later you may call back asking for potential job information and leads. Information interviews are a great way to network, one of the skills that will be discussed later in this book. The more people you know, the greater your sources of information about the world. Information interviews are a passport to greater experience and awareness of the world, but many people are too frightened to try this harmless and cost-free way of getting ahead. The younger you are when you start doing them, the greater your rewards will be.

One Student's Impressions of a Speechwriter. Irene O'Donnell, an English major at UIC, was interested in becoming a speechwriter. She wrote the following report after her information interview:

> This past week I interviewed Ms. Angeline Harris,* a woman with extensive experience in speechwriting. She passed along some very enlightening information about this field, which I will try to summarize.
>
> Speechwriting for money never occurs right away, and according to Ms. Harris, most speechwriters never intended to work in this area for a living. Instead, it usually happens as an offshoot of something else.
>
> The two career paths that lead to this field are politics or public relations. By following a candidate for some time in another capacity or working as a political journalist, political speechwriting can eventually follow.
>
> The majority of corporate speechwriting happens in the PR department. Ms. Harris advised starting out at a large agency with a variety of clients to develop the kind of experience that can lead to speechwriting. However, even with a great resume Ms. Harris told me that once she began writing speeches on a freelance basis, it was still very difficult for her to gain contacts and further work outside of the clients she maintained from her PR job.
>
> In order to write a good speech, she said that one needs to be able "to write a good pro-

*not person's real name

motional schtick." She finds speechwriting unfulfilling and views it more as a way to increase her income. She suggested browsing through trade journals about PR and business writing on the Internet for more information.

On a different note, Ms. Harris told me that although she earned a fantastic salary working in the PR field, she found it extremely unsatisfying. She described such work as "Not the way writers would naturally live," and advised me to take care; that as an English major, whatever I start out my career in, I will very likely become quite stuck in. Several years down the road, changing my career would be extremely difficult, if not virtually impossible. She encouraged me to strive for personal satisfaction before salary. If I do that, she was confident that I would be fine.

On a final note, Ms. Harris told me that if I wanted to do an internship at her former PR company, which has an office here in Chicago, she would put in a good word for me.

Spotlights: Testing Services

Private Testing Services

Private testing services charge a fee to test your aptitudes. They are listed in the yellow pages of your phone book under "Educational Testing Services." If you are interested, call each one, request their materials, and make an appointment so you can compare what different companies have to offer.

As an example, the nationwide Johnson O'Connor Research Foundation offers testing for eighteen distinct aptitudes and compares the results with aptitudes required in hundreds of different careers. The company says that its tests measure inherent abilities that have little to do with knowledge, culture, interests, or experience.

Among the tests offered are personality, either objective or subjective. The company reports that three-quarters of the people tested are objective, that is, generalists. The other 25 percent view their work as extensions of themselves, preferring to work alone.

Another ability measured is foresight, the ability to work toward a long-term goal. If a person scores low on this measurement, he or she needs to break up tasks into manageable parts. A high score is interpreted to mean that the person will have no problem staying with careers that require many years, such as medicine, research, or space exploration.

Ideaphoria, or creative imagination, is measured for the person's ability to think of new ways to accomplish a task. In accounting or engineering a high ideaphoria skill is not needed; in advertising, politics, and journalism, Johnson O'Connor says it's important.

The tests also measure structural visualization, abstract thinking, inductive and analytical reasoning, memory, and auditory and motor aptitudes, as well as vocabulary, the only learned ability the organization considers.

After completing this battery of tests, which takes approximately seven hours, a counselor describes your profile of abilities and careers that would fit well with this profile. The tests and the consultation cost approximately $400.

The company says that the tests for many people merely confirm what they had suspected were their strengths. For these people the test results seem to give them added ammunition to pursue certain goals.

The people who have the most trouble with the results are those who have strengths in many different categories. Because their aptitude is strong everywhere, it is difficult for them to decide which avenue to pursue.

Computerized Testing Services

Many campuses offer computerized programs that you can follow at your own leisure to determine your career path. One that is used on many campuses is called SIGI-Plus (System of Interactive Guidance and Information Plus More), a program designed by the Educational Testing Service. Colleges subscribe to the program, paying a monthly fee for students to be able to use the test.

Colleges offer SIGI-Plus to their students as an interactive aid for the main aspects of career decision making and planning. When you finish the test, you will be given a printout of the conclusions gathered as a result of your responses.

The first section of the test introduces you to the program and outlines what it will do for you. Next, you answer questions about self-awareness: What do I want? What am I good at? This part helps you decide what's really important to you by identifying your most important values, interests, and skills.

The next part of the test focuses on occupations. You can choose from a menu the characteristics you want in your work and what you want to avoid in your work. The program then lists occupations that match what you asked for. This part helps you to select a college major and see a list of related occupations.

Next, you choose hypothetical occupations and the program tells you what skills these occupations require. Further, you learn the possibilities for advancement in these fields and the potential income. Also, you will learn the national employment outlook in each field as well as the educational requirements.

Can I do what's required? is an important question, and the program lists the skills of various occupations and gives you a chance to rate yourself on these skills. It also informs you of typical preparation paths to the occupations. Courses and course descriptions are listed, allowing you to consider whether you want to tackle the courses required for preparation in any field.

Coping is an important ingredient in any decision about a college major. This part of the program will help you determine whether your time-management skills are adequate for a particular career, and how well you will deal with competition, using computers, and doing math, if it is required.

The program explores what's right for you in terms of rewards and chances of getting in, as well as whether an occupation is a good choice with all things considered. Finally, the program gives you a plan of action in light of what you have discovered through answering all the questions.

Reviewing the results with a counselor will bring out many aspects of the process that you might not consider on your own.

Flashlights: Independent Educational Consultants

In the phone book you can find the names of independent educational consultants who specialize in the college choice process. Their current fees range from $1,000 to $3,500 depending on the area of the country. They review transcripts and test scores, recommend test preparations, if needed, and answer questions about majors and what colleges have to offer. They also help students develop ideas for essays.

The good ones visit several colleges a year, meeting with administrators to discover changes in curriculum and what the colleges are expecting of students. They are quick to spot new trends in admissions and offerings of new programs. "We're the ones who warn students not to blow off senior year," said Sue Bigg, a consultant in Chicago.

Tasks to Get You to Your Major

4

Take charge. Letting a major rise to the surface without effort on your part leaves too much to chance. With a small amount of work each semester on the subject of choosing a major, you will be better informed and armed to make the right choice. "I wish I had known" are words of futility after you have spent four or more years on a subject only to find you would have been happier with another major. And remember, a major isn't forever.

A Working Calendar for High School Students

Freshman Year

The main task freshman year is adjusting to high school. So much is new—you may never have changed classes before, or may be surprised at how much is expected of you. Just finding the right people to have lunch with can be stressful. Whatever discomfort level you experience

69

this year, it will get better. The main task is to concentrate on learning how to learn. Most students gain expertise on studying during this year. As you learn how to study your grades will improve. If you have time, joining school clubs is an excellent way to meet new people and to find people to study with.

Sophomore Year

Sophomore year is the least stressful of all four years and a good opportunity to learn how to interact with teachers. If you have not yet met the college counselors, now is the time to introduce yourself. While freshman year was a time of disorientation, most sophomores are beginning to feel more confident and more able to talk with teachers and other people to gain information. The sooner you learn this skill of reaching out to people who have more experience than you, the quicker you will find useful information.

This is a good year to try different activities. If you have always been very active socially, it's a good time to try some quiet pursuits that you can accomplish on your own. If you've always been a person who stays to himself or herself, this is the year to spread your wings. Take some chances, try talking to people you haven't talked with before. They may surprise you. If they don't seem interested in talking, move on to someone else. It's their loss. Be alert to news of college fairs, programs on college admissions, and books or magazine articles about people in professions that are of interest to you.

Junior Year

In junior year, your life will be dominated by tests. You will probably take the SAT I and/or the ACT in the spring and the SAT II, if required by the schools you are considering. You will be taking the PSAT/NMSQT, which may qualify you for National Merit Scholarship awards.

You will probably be scheduled for a meeting with your college counselor to review your transcript and standardized test scores. At this meeting you will learn what colleges will be interested in accepting you. College representatives will be making the rounds. This is a good time to ask them about specific programs that interest you.

Other students will start talking about where they are thinking of going to college. At a school where many students are college bound, the jockeying for status starts early. At schools where few are going to college, the decision is difficult because there are few other students with whom to share ideas and information. If possible, schedule trips to campuses on days when schools are in session. Start listening more carefully to people already out of college. Ask them questions about their jobs. Ask what they majored in in college. A good question to ask is, Would they major in that same subject again?

Senior Year

Senior year is a scramble. Prepare the summer before senior year by spending time at the library or at Web sites reading about what majors different colleges have to offer. Also spend time reading about the majors in different books, magazines, and on-line. Read the *Occupational Outlook Handbook* compiled by the U.S. Department of Labor, Bureau of Labor Statistics. The government gathers information from trade associations, professional societies, unions, and industrial organizations to provide up-to-date information on jobs and the projections of employment in these jobs over a ten-year period. The highlights of the government's information are provided in Chapter 9 of this book. Be sure and look also at Chapter 7 in this book called "The New, Unusual, and Design-Your-Own Majors." Then look at the colleges you are considering to see if they provide you with a wide choice of alternatives.

A Working Calendar for College Students

Having a schedule of what you need to do each semester of college will help keep you advancing toward your goal.

Freshman Year

1. Take as diverse a selection of courses as you can. If electives are available to you, study your choices carefully and consider studying something you have no exposure to, such as psychology.

2. Find out where the Career Counseling Center is on campus. Just know where it is, you don't have to go there.

3. Build your social skills so that you learn to talk to people easily and can get valuable information from them.

4. In reading newspapers and magazines note what jobs people do and what the stories tell you about the jobs.

Sophomore Year

1. Now that everything has settled down and you are comfortable being a college student, review all the courses offered at your college. This sounds like an amazingly simple and time-wasting exercise, but you will be surprised at the diversity and richness of courses offered at most colleges and universities today. Students frequently suffer, like the rest of the population, from nearsightedness, only focusing on their field of study. It's important to review all your options.

2. Find upperclasspeople who are majoring in the subjects you are interested in. They will tell you the realities of the course of study.

3. Even if your mind is made up about your major, consider the course sequences for two others. Also, consider what you might want to minor in. Minors frequently are overlooked and can be a source of great interest.

4. Find out who does the advising at your school. Make an appointment with this person early second semester. The school may already have you scheduled to see the advisor sometime during the year. Be sure you bring a notebook and have prepared many questions. These people are extremely busy and you want to make the most of the time they have.

5. Play the "What if" game with yourself. "What if I majored in geology and minored in business?" The purpose is to discover what kind of expertise this will give you after you finish college.

6. Declare your major and minor or your double major. Register for as many courses as you can in your major and minor for the summer and fall. By taking advanced courses early, you will determine whether you have made the right choice or not.

Junior Year

1. Work very hard in your courses so that your grade point average in your major is high. Frequently employers ask the overall grade point average and the grade point average in your major.

2. Start getting to know the professors in your major department by stopping in during office hours and asking them questions. The main purpose is to gain information and for them to remember you when it

comes time to write letters of recommendation for jobs or graduate school. Remember the Maytag ad featuring the lonely repairman? That's how many instructors feel during office hours when no one shows up. They have a wealth of information in their fields and most are willing to share if students show an interest. Inquire about research projects they are doing in which you may get involved.

3. Find out how students participate in internship or cooperative education projects at your school. Sign up for one during the year and for one next summer.

4. Be alert to people with your major who are working so that you may interview them about their jobs.

5. Go to job fairs to get an idea of what they offer.

6. Check with your major advisor to make sure you are taking the courses required in your major for graduation.

Senior Year

1. Make an appointment early in the year with the Career Center on campus.

2. Conduct information interviews with people in your field who are working.

3. Spend sufficient time to write and rewrite an impressive resume. The Career Center on campus will have books, classes, and staff to help with this task.

4. Collect names of people who can be used for references in your job search, or faculty who would be willing to write letters of recommendation for you for graduate school.

5. Go to job fairs to familiarize yourself with what opportunities are available for you and to distribute your resume to prospective employers.

6. Master the art of writing cover letters to go with your resume. These letters are a sales tool to convince prospective employers of your desirability as an employee.

This rough outline of a calendar for four years of college will give you an idea of the time when each major task should be accomplished.

Building Networks

If you hang around with only your roommate from freshman year to graduation (highly unlikely), you will not know much about what the world of majors has to offer. Frequently, it's difficult to meet someone who is considering a major in nursing if you are on the engineering track. The engineers benefit from meeting nursing majors and philosophy majors can learn from the computer scientists. And vice versa.

Even if you are quite confident about what you want to study, exposure to other people's interests can make you change your mind. Frequently, students choose a major because of family pressure or underexposure to fields available to them.

If you are naturally social and eager to meet others, you are already well on your way to meeting people on campus who will expand your thinking about majors. If you have not developed your social skills yet, college is a perfect time to start.

In almost every campus scenario there is a chance to meet new people—the cafeteria, the shuttle bus stop, in the lecture hall, playing soccer. It's not unreasonable to set a goal of meeting one new person a day. Most schools are in session about eight months. Eight times 30 days equals 240 new people you could meet. What a wealth of information! This process is not going to happen by itself unless you set a goal of being open to meeting new people. They will immeasurably enrich your life.

Learning to Initiate Small Talk

The process of conversation does not start with big ideas. Usually people start with small subjects like lunch, team scores, the unreliability of the bus schedule. Then, after both people check out the other person's language use, level of sophistication, attitude, and other clues, the conversation either proceeds or it stops. Sometimes, it is merely a time filler.

Small talk is extremely important in the process of getting information you need about your major and your subsequent career. Believe it or not, people will judge your sophistication by how well you are able to talk about nothing of importance. Frequently, this talk revolves around sports, the weather, or food. Other popular topics are trying to stay in shape, the development of characters on "ER," and overspending on credit cards. Almost everyone in America knows something about one of these topics. People who win the lottery and what happens to them also brings out conversation.

College is a great place to start practicing the art of saying nothing of substance. Many famous people have developed this to an art form: professional athletes, politicians in response to reporters' probing questions, most presidents of the United States. If you prove expert at saying nothing, while at the same time being congenial, people will guess that you really know some important things that you aren't ready to divulge.

Listen to the small talk that goes on around you every day.

"Hi! How's it going? Can you believe this weather?"
"Yeh, and I still don't have boots."

"Well, hi there. How's the semester going?"
"Not too bad, but I have this calculus class that's a killer."

"Hi! What's happening?"
"Not much, but I got a flat tire on the way to school today."

Imagine that you have to add the third sentence to any of these exchanges. What direction could you go?

Most small talk involves keeping the tennis ball in play, quite often effectively by merely asking a question that hinges on the last statement. By listening to what other people say, you can easily develop a repertoire of small talk. Just copy.

Bypassing Procrastination

Procrastination is another word for perfectionism. Procrastinators have huge imaginations of how grand any project could be, then don't get started because they can never attain such heights. As one junior remarked, "I finally figured it out. It doesn't matter how smart you are, what matters is whether you can stay on top of everything that needs to get done." A sure way not to stay on top is to avoid doing tasks because you've imagined how extraordinary they have to be. Settle for ordinary. If you have extra time, then maybe you can try for extraordinary. Avoid the procrastination trap.

Doing Your Homework on Majors

Choosing a major requires homework, footwork, earwork, voicework. Similar to the homework you've been doing since second grade, it requires preparation, organization, attack!

The College Admissions Office at your school has several of the books that list the facts about schools. You may decide to buy one for review at home. As you look through this list, jot down the names and addresses of the schools that interest you. Your advisor may have some information about the schools that is not apparent in reading the books. Other sources of information are described in the following sections.

College Catalogues

While Web sites are popular, the only real source of reliable information is the catalogue provided by each college. The Web sites of colleges have disclaimers: "Remember, this electronic message is not the official policy of this college." Consult the college catalogue for accurate information. Libraries frequently keep copies of college catalogues, sometimes only on microfiche. Having your own copy leaves you free to refer to it often and mark questions and comments in the margins.

Keep a list of the catalogues you have requested. Depending on what time of year your request is made, delivery may take as much as two months, but more typically, a month.

As the catalogues come in, check them off on your list. Writing your own scoring system of the news offered in the catalogues is helpful. At the top of your grid, write or type the features that are important to you, such as geographic location, size, ratio of men to women, tuition, financial aid, whatever you have decided is important. On the left-hand side of the page, write the names of the schools.

Naturally, schools design these catalogues to attract students. They are not as polished yet as advertising tools, but they do represent an effort on the schools' part to get you interested.

Some points to consider when looking at the catalogues:

What has the school chosen to emphasize?

What majors does it offer?

Which majors are of interest to you?

What courses are listed under the major?

Do the course descriptions sound interesting?

What kind of people are represented in the pictures?
Are there pictures of women as well as men in the

science and engineering labs? Are minorities represented in the pictures?

Do the students in the pictures look like the kind of people you want to be with?

What is the spirit of the catalogue? Is it nuts and bolts or are there creative descriptions of the process of education?

The Library

Where else to go but the library to find information? The library is the repository for everything you ever wanted to know about majors. Talk with the reference librarian about the areas you want to search. Many college libraries have special sections designed for finding information about majors and their relationship to careers.

The Computer

Although Web sites for colleges and departments are evolving and not all are in place and working as viable information storehouses, they are a place where you can search for information. A complete listing of college Web sites is available by using a search engine such as Yahoo! or Altavista: http://www.yahoo.com or http://www.altavista.digital.com. Once you reach one of these, type in the name of the college or university and the word "admissions." Click the submit or search button. Most college and university Web sites have a hyper-text table of contents for you to find a specific department.

Other sites to start at are Peterson's "Education and Career Center," located at http://www.petersons.com. The Internet University-Educational Web sites can be found at http://www.caso.com/iu/research/web.html. Using Netscape, pull down "file," click "open location" and insert this address, or replace your "location" line with this address and hit return.

The Crucial Campus Visit

After you have established as much as you can by reading the catalogues, prepare for a visit to the campus. Schools are eager to have you visit. Your visit is going to include more than following a talking leader around the buildings. You are going to request interviews with students and professors in the major you are considering. A campus visit will be much more meaningful if you actually get a chance to ask people questions about the subject you are considering studying.

Using the techniques you learned earlier in informational interviews, you will prepare questions such as the following:

What will I learn in this major?

What are the strengths of the professors in this major?

How does a major at this school differ from the same major at other schools?

Are there opportunities for field study or internships?

Are classes in my major hard to get into?

What do students with this major do for a living after they graduate?

What is the most difficult class in this major?

What are typical minors that students in this major have chosen?

Is there an opportunity to do an interdisciplinary major with this major?

Is there opportunity for foreign travel with this major?

In this major, how many years does it typically take to graduate?

What are the most popular courses in this major?

What skills do you need to have to do well in this major?

At what stage of my college career do I have to declare this major?

Is it competitive to get accepted into the department?

What grade point average is required?

Where are most of the classes in this major held on campus?

Is it possible for me to sit in on a class? (Request this ahead of time.)

What skills will I have upon completion of this major?

How long has this been a major on this campus?

Is there any thought of eliminating or merging this major with another discipline in the near future?

Is the school sensitive to language barriers on the part of its teaching assistants?

Are the teaching assistants evaluated for their teaching by the faculty?

How much access will I have to full faculty members?

What is a typical course of study each year in this major?

Faculty members sit through dozens of such interviews each year and appreciate the student who has his or her questions ready. Often, the discussion will veer off into other areas of interest, but at least you will have a solid foundation of questions answered when you leave.

Some of the questions above are better answered by an upperclassperson who has learned the ropes. It's best to get answers from both faculty and students to get a complete picture of what a major will mean at this school.

If you are one of the many people who are looking at schools and don't have a particular major in mind yet, these are the questions you should be asking:

When do I have to declare a major?

Does each department have a grade point average requirement?

The Campus Bookstore

Campus bookstores contain a wealth of information. They are divided alphabetically into subject areas, with all the books required for each course arranged by course number on the shelves. Some courses have no books because the instructor prefers to use course packets of copied articles with copyright permission bound together for course reading and discussion.

Look at the books required for the courses. The books will give you a sense of the many aspects of the course, such as degree of complexity and amount of reading required, as well as your own familiarity with the material. And of course, watch out for sticker shock. College books are very expensive today, with undergraduates having $200 to $350 book bills each semester. Parents urge students to buy used books, but because of the information explosion many books are out of date very quickly and the instructor opts for the latest edition.

Volunteering

Offering to work without pay can open doors. Many places that do exciting work will gladly accept your services for free. In return, you get a chance to see how this organization works and whether it's appealing as a place to spend your career. Formerly, the only place young people could volunteer was as "candy stripers" or some such name, wheeling people around or pushing the book cart in a hospital. Today, the world of the volunteer has greatly expanded and offers people access to many places of work.

The second advantage of volunteering is the people you meet who can steer you to other opportunities. One student volunteered for the campus-sponsored Habitat for Humanity, the group that helps people build their own homes. While hammering away she met an editor for a business publication. When a job opened up, he suggested that she submit her resume, which led to a job after graduation.

Whether it's driving the night ministry bus or conducting tours of a botanical garden, volunteerism adds a dimension to your life beyond the classroom. One student who worked on a rape victims' phone line said she never realized before the extent to which women are devalued in society. And, she said, she was left wondering, why do we put up with it? The volunteer conducting tours at the botanical garden might become interested in the emerging field of the medicinal possibilities of plants.

Internships

At most schools you start internships after your sophomore year. Working usually ten to fifteen hours a week during the school year, students gain needed experience in their field before graduation. No longer is a college degree by itself considered sufficient preparation for the world of work. Employers look for experience on the resume.

Besides working for an organization, many internships require students to submit written material about their experience, either in the form of a journal or in research papers written about the internship. The professor supervising the internship details what should be included in the journal. Typical topics, written about weekly, are:

1. How I interact with other people at the internship
2. Skills I am developing at the internship
3. Observations about conflict management
4. Workplace politics
5. I like going to my internship because . . .
6. On days when I don't feel like going to the internship it's usually because . . .
7. Suggestions I could make to improve the functioning of my unit
8. What I have observed about team dynamics
9. Traits of people who are effective at work
10. Traits of people who are ineffective at work
11. If I were supervising interns, I'd . . .

Research papers about the internship might be:

1. An analysis of the audience or clients of the organization
2. An interview with someone other than the intern's supervisor who can give an overall view of the goals and plans of the organization
3. A short report on the culture of the organization, featuring what is valued there
4. A long report on the relationship of the organization to its competition

Students may get college credit for completing an internship. Some are paid and others pay only a stipend for travel expenses.

Another type of experiential learning is the cooperative education experience, or co-op. Names such as internship and co-op have become intermingled, but generally co-op jobs are paid. Frequently, students do not receive college credit for them.

Katherine's Internship Journal

Katherine Nelson, an English major, worked as a public relations intern for a major cellular services company during two summers. Then she was hired to work each Friday during the school year. Here are comments she wrote in her internship journal.

My first summer was great, but this past summer was even better. Some of the projects I worked on included: writing press releases, organizing employee off-site meetings, participating on the company's Internet Task Force, editing the customer newsletter, and other vital public relations activities. Out of all of these my favorite task was working on the redesign of the Internet site.

I was in charge of getting all the press releases on the site. I also had to make sure each and every product name had been trademarked on our site. For this I had to work with the legal department of the corporation. That took a lot of patience.

I have to commend the company for its excellent internship program. They treat the interns royally. This past summer there were seventeen of us, most of us from UIC. We had an orientation day, two lunches with the president of the company, a tour of a technical site, and a final event, which was both fun and painful.

We played Whirlybird. The basics of the game were you sit in a bumper car and you wear a mitt. The object is for your team to get the ball into the basket. I walked away with two huge bruises on my legs but overall it was a lot of fun. Afterwards we had lunch in a restaurant by the office where each intern received a plaque and a whole duffel bag of the company's products.

The company president strongly believes in teamwork. I think this notion of teamwork helps the environment of the office. It builds relationships not just based on work but also on friendship. As I mentioned in class one day, associates go out all the time after work to bars or they work out together in the Wellness Center. . . .

After ordering out Chinese food with the rest of the department I spent some time working with the trademark attorney. I never knew it took so long to trademark and make sure something was legally correct. I'm just glad it's done.

Then I moved on to looking at some customer letters. This week I just organized them, I didn't have time to start writing form letters. There are so many things I want to get done and that need to be done. I want to write form letters in response to customers who write letters, organize and establish a system for storing old press releases, and finish a new media kit. I continued my work on the media kit today but didn't get much done because binders needed to go out in the evening mail. So I had to put everything down and help with the crisis. . . .

I didn't go into work this Friday because I'm loaded with papers to do for the end of the semester. I hate telling them I can't come in, I feel they might think I don't care or that I don't have any type of responsibility. But, if I don't graduate I won't be able to get a job anywhere, except maybe at the corner Walgreen's or McDonald's. I haven't spent my parents' valuable money to go to work behind a cash register. Like my mom said, they have to understand that you are still in school and that it is your number one priority. I just hope they realize that. . . .

My dream would be to continue working here as a full-time employee or as an associate. I forgot to write that I have been receiving the most unusual stuff in the mail; it's from the company's Retirement Foundation. I will have to call someone and let them know that I am only an intern.

Contacting Professional Associations

Many professions have associations to keep their members informed on the latest trends affecting their jobs and also to give young people who are thinking of joining this profession information about what the jobs involve. You can look up the association's address in the library or find its Web page on the Internet to learn more about each one. Most of those you contact will provide you with brochures and fact sheets about the profession. You also should ask about upcoming seminars in your city sponsored by the association. It is another great way to network with people who are already in the field that interests you. Check the list of professional associations in Chapter 11.

Your Part-Time Job   Deciding on a major involves talking to experts, hearing advice, keeping notes, and reading about occupations. Think of all this work as your part-time job. Going to school is your day job. Every day you check off a few more tasks so that you don't get overwhelmed with the whole process. A phone call to set up an information interview, a quick stop at the college counseling office, just do a little every day.

Descriptions of Majors from College Catalogues

Majors mean much more than their names imply. While "geography" may sound like looking at a globe and memorizing the names of nations, today it includes the study of terrain, natural resources and implications for ownership of these resources, developing skills in map reading and design, and aerial photo interpretation.

As you will see when you read the college catalogues, some colleges go to great lengths to describe what a major at their school is, others merely list what the requirements for a particular major are. Listed below are descriptions of majors as written by the colleges noted. This list will give you an idea of what you can expect in studying a particular major. Philosophies and approaches will vary from school to school. This is a good chapter to read if you have no idea of what your major will be. It's also a good source for broadening your understanding of majors. You might find one here to investigate further.

Anthropology   Anthropology is the study of human cultural diversity as it has developed over time and through space, as well as in relation to biology and the environment. The aim of the program is to provide students a strong foundation in the main subfields of anthropology—including cultural anthropology (the study of contemporary cultures and social organization), archaeology (the study of cultures and social organization of the past), physical anthropology (human biological diversity, both in comparative perspective and as it has developed over time), and anthropological linguistics (the relationship of language to culture and social organization). Advanced courses as well as independent research allow majors to focus their studies in preparation for a wide range of careers, both in anthropology itself as well as in other professional fields, including international education, law, medicine, social work, public health, urban planning, forensics, and cultural resource management. (Beloit College, Beloit, WI)

Art   Usually this major includes two parts: studio art and art history, combining performance and study. Art majors are encouraged to study abroad for a semester or a year. The Department of Art provides curricular opportunities for the development of technical skills, aesthetic judgment, and historical understanding. Participation in both studio and art-history courses stimulates critical thinking and refines creative potentials in the visual arts. The Permanent Collection of original works of art, especially works on paper in the print and Drawing Study Room, supplements formal course study. (Grinnell College, Grinnell, IA)

Biology   Recent dramatic progress in our understanding of the nature of life has revolutionized the science of biology. Applications of the methods, concepts, and approaches of modern mathematics, physics, chemistry, and information science are providing deep insight into basic biological problems such as the manner in which genes and viruses replicate themselves; the control of gene expression in cells; the regulation of cellular activity; the mechanisms of growth and development; and the nature and interactions of nerve activity, brain function, and behavior. Qualified experimental and computational biologists will find opportunities for challenging work in basic research as well as in medicine and in biotechnology. (California Institute of Technology, Pasadena, CA)

Business Administration

The Center for Business and Economics is dedicated to preparing its students for successful careers in a global economy characterized by complex issues, ambiguity and change. A key belief underlying the Center's programs is that success in business generally depends on specialized skills; awareness and understanding beyond a field of specialization; plus such personal attributes as leadership skills, adaptability, healthy self-esteem, competency in problem solving and the ability to communicate effectively. The Center affords the opportunity for each student to develop these skills, perspectives and personal attributes, recognizing that students come to the program with differing needs and expectations. (Elmhurst College, Elmhurst, IL)

Chemistry

Members of the Department engage in extensive research programs in the areas of experimental and theoretical analytical, biological, inorganic, organic, physical and polymer chemistry. Research activities involve the synthesis and characterization of new solid state materials, development of new analytical methods, including methods for separations and purification, characterization of new and known materials by spectroscopic and other physical methods, synthesis and applications of new materials in catalysis and related areas, and chemistry and photochemistry of organic and bioorganic materials. (University of Connecticut, Storrs, CT)

Classics

The study of classics focuses on stimulating and important concepts that, originally defined and refined by classical authors, lead to an increased awareness of the complexities of a nation's culture, its institutions, and its underlying values. Freedom, justice, absolute and relative moral values, and the role of the individual in society are still issues of great concern today and are the touchstones by which we measure the accomplishments of civilization. Students of the classics analyze these and other themes of classical literature in the context of their continuing intellectual and emotional influence on Western civilization and the modern world. To this end, students of the classics study the languages of ancient Greece and Rome. Beginning, intermediate, and advanced courses in such authors as Homer, Sophocles, Plato, Cicero, Virgil, and Augustine provide students with the opportunity to examine the contributions of these seminal thinkers to the intellectual traditions of the Western world. (Syracuse University, Syracuse NY)

Communication

Students in communication arts and sciences study the process by which messages are devised and disseminated. Attention is given to the various roles and stages in the communication process. The contexts of communication, from interpersonal communication to mass communication, are analyzed and distinguished. As a crossroads discipline, communication is studied from both the humanities and social science perspectives. The study of communication is built around a framework that allows for an understanding of theory, opportunity for criticism of messages, and practice and research in the discipline.

Students will study a wide range of communication areas, including speech communication and rhetoric, interpersonal communication, mass communication, theatre and voice science.

Communication students can apply their understanding of this vital process in a variety of fields such as corporate communication, public relations, personnel, advertising, marketing, law, mass media, sales, public service and the performing arts. (DePauw University, Greencastle, IN)

Computer Science

The Computer Science Program is designed to meet the broad needs of students in a liberal arts environment. Computer science students learn to write programs well, but the fundamental objective of the program is to provide a broader perspective: the science of computing. The focus of the computer science program is to investigate the power, the limitations, and the applications of computing. The current computer science offerings are designed to meet the needs of students whose fields of interest include the following:

1. Computer Science. The computer science major offers a solid preparation for graduate school. Students interested in this track usually do independent projects and write a thesis.

2. Philosophy and Psychology. The field of computer science investigates many of the same questions found in these sister fields, but from a different perspective. Students of the philosophy of the mind or the psychology of vision can sharpen their arguments by including artificial intelligence and computer vision in their curriculum.

3. Economics, Management, Mathematics and the Sciences. As computers make their way into our everyday lives, managers should have a working knowledge of computer science to make quality decisions about how to use computers in their operations. Economists, mathematicians, and scientists are increasingly using computers as a modeling tool in their research. (Mount Holyoke College, South Hadley, MA)

Criminal Justice

Criminal Justice is a social and behavioral science field of study that selects crime, law, and the criminal justice system for its subject matter. Using social science methodology, the program examines the occurrence of crimes in various settings and society's organized response to them. The response includes the investigation of crimes and arrest of offenders by the police, and their prosecution, defense, and adjudication by the courts; it also examines the role of judges and the probation officers and an array of sentencing and correctional outcomes. In addition, it treats the legal system's noncriminal functions as well as efforts by local communities to resolve disputes and control crime.

The degree prepares graduates for a broad range of professional roles in the criminal justice system, as well as the broader legal system. It also serves as entry to graduate programs of criminal justice and related research and professional programs such as law, sociology, public policy and other social services. (The University of Illinois at Chicago)

Economics

Economics is a fascinating and challenging social science discipline because it deals with such vital current problems as inflation, unemployment, monopoly, economic growth, pollution, and poverty. These are problems that fill our newspapers and pervade our politics. They affect us as members of society concerned with how our economic system functions, and as individuals concerned with jobs, wages, taxes, and the cost of living. Economists seek to understand these problems by developing a systematic and thorough understanding of precisely how the economic system operates, including the mechanisms by which resources are allocated, prices determined, income redistributed, and economic development achieved. The approach of the modern economist is primarily analytical but tempered with historical, institutional, and statistical data. The analytical method of economics recognizes that various choices are open to a society in solving its economic problems. Students are often attracted to economics as a discipline precisely because they want to be able to understand current trends and evaluate the effects of alternative policies. They soon discover, however, that there are no simple answers to the problems of allocating resources among competing uses. To begin to approach these problems as an economist requires an understanding of economic theory, methods and approaches, and applied fields.

A major in economics is good preparation for graduate work in a number of areas: law, public policy, public administration, business, industrial relations, international relations, urban and regional planning, and environmental studies. (University of Wisconsin, Madison)

Education

With an understanding that the importance of intelligent, caring, and creative teachers is crucial to the well being of our society, the education department prepares students to become effective teachers across the age continuum from early childhood through young adulthood.

The combination of sound academic standards, broad liberal education, emphasis on subject preparation and thorough grounding in the study of education as an art, science, and mission results in the development of graduates of outstanding promise as teachers. Additionally, education courses provide opportunities for liberal arts students, regardless of academic or professional interests, to critically and creatively reflect on contemporary societal concerns regarding children and youth, and the status of national and international educational systems.

The curriculum is centered in four mutually supportive themes:

Social Advocacy. John Dewey stated, "Education is the fundamental method of social progress and reform." These words assume special significance at a time when there is widespread recognition that current social and educational policies and practices designed to fulfill the needs and aspirations of children and youth are in crisis. In response, the curriculum is designed to promote social responsibility (including preparation for social service and social leadership) and cultural pluralism (including concern for gender, race, class, international and urban issues), especially as these commitments contribute to the advancement of social, political, and educational welfare of children and youth.

Life Span Development. In order to address the needs and aspirations of children and youth, the curriculum reflects current theory and research, which articulates a developmental continuum of human learning, growth, change, crisis and renewal. The study of human development is conducted in an inclusive and integrative manner, addressing patterns and processes across the domains of cognitive, affective, intuitive, social, physical, and moral growth, and throughout the age continuum from early childhood through young adulthood. The educational implications of individual variations in intellectual, emotional, and physical capabilities and factors related to gender, class, race, or cultural heritage are also addressed. Additionally, the interplay among developmental processes on personal, organizational, and societal levels is carefully considered.

Cultural Pluralism. The curriculum further reflects commitment to the concept of human diversity as a *resource* to schools and society. It is assumed that both special challenges and unique opportunities are associated with individual variations in intellectual, emotional, and physical capabilities and factors related to gender, class, race, and cultural heritage. Students are expected to assess implications of their own cultural heritage, to grow in understanding and compassion as they explore the perspectives of others, and to act upon their growing awareness in supportive and life-enhancing ways.

Experiential Learning. The curriculum is further designed to ensure ongoing and developmentally appropriate opportunities for application, integration, and evaluation of educational theory and practice. In doing so the curriculum promotes understanding of development-in-context, thereby acknowledging the dynamic and complex constellation of factors and relationships that contribute to the educational process. A developmental sequence of field experience is integrated throughout education course work beginning with opportunities to develop observational skills, then to participate in activities that support instruction, and finally, to assume instructional roles. Each student's field work is structured to ensure opportunities to interact with students across the age spectrum from early childhood through adolescence before selecting an age for specialization. Field experiences are further structured to include experiences with exceptional students and work in pluralistic educational settings. (Macalester College, Saint Paul, MN)

Engineering

Engineering is a professional field that influences almost every element of our society. Perhaps no other profession is more truly concerned with the safety of health and property. The goals of the engineering profession—maintenance of high ethical standards and quality performance—are integral to the academic programs in all Schools of Engineering.

A student is expected to graduate with a solid technical background that will enable him or her to take a positive place in society and contribute to finding solutions to the complex problems facing our nation. (Purdue University, West Lafayette, IN)

English

The functions of the Department of English are: first, to help all students of the university to achieve proficiency in mature reading, writing and thinking skills; second, to help English majors and minors develop a critical appreciation for literary content and form and an understanding of the structure and history of the language; third, to prepare English majors and minors for teaching and non-teaching careers and to provide them with a sound basis for advanced study; fourth, to provide courses in both expository writing and creative writing; fifth, to teach remedial courses for native speakers with language difficulties, to provide special courses for international students, and to furnish all students with the services of a writing center; sixth, to create an atmosphere that encourages appreciation and understanding of our richly diverse literary heritage and its relationship to contemporary personal and cultural problems; seventh, to offer to the community the services of the department in developing courses especially designed for continuing education. (St. Cloud State University, St. Cloud, MN)

Environmental Design

As population density increases and natural resources are depleted and squandered, decisions affecting the sustainability and aesthetics of the land and other natural resources assume increased importance. Both the public and the private sectors must be involved if the challenge of balancing development pressures with environmental protection interests is to be realized. Traditionally, opportunities for specific professional involvement have been found in the fields of architecture, landscape architecture, and regional planning. Additional professional opportunities are available in the fields of horticulture, environmental law, real estate development, and many other disciplines that share an environmental concern. For professionals in related fields such as law, education, community development or finance, the sound theoretical understanding of environmental issues gained through the environmental design program contributes to and informs land use decision making processes and values. (University of Massachusetts, Amherst, MA)

French

Beyond providing mastery of the language skills (listening, speaking, reading, writing) of modern French needed for all purposes of daily life, the major introduces students to a central tradition of Western and indeed world culture. Since the Middle Ages, French literature, thought, taste, and art have helped shape the essential experience and self-understanding of humanity at large. Survey courses and upper-division seminars offer a range of exposures to the French cultural past and the far-flung ethnic and national diversity of the French-speaking present, exploring such distinctively French contributions to world culture as: Arthurian romance, troubadour poetry, and Gothic architecture; the love sonnets of the Pleiade, the comic novels of Rabelais, and the essays of Montaigne; the neoclassical theatre of Corneille, Moliere, and Racine and the critical philosophy of Descartes and Pascal; the Enlightenment philosophies of Voltaire, Diderot, and Rousseau; the psychological refinements of French fiction from Mme de La Fayette to Proust; artistic revolutions like impressionism and surrealism; the renewal of artistic conventions in the Theatre of the Absurd, the New Novel, and the cinema of the New Wave; the French-language literature of Africa, Canada, and the Caribbean; and the vital presence of French writers in major movements of twentieth-century thought like existentialism, structuralism, feminism, psychoanalysis, and contemporary cultural studies and multiculturalism.

In pursuing an undergraduate degree in French, majors are expected to acquire the following forms of knowledge:

- an awareness of the fundamental outlines of the history of French literature from the Middle Ages to the present;

- Familiarity with significant works of French literature and awareness of the literary culture of the French-speaking world;

- awareness of the historical context in which particular works were written and of the relation between literature and other forms of cultural expression (e.g., art, philosophy, politics, religion)

- awareness of contemporary French culture, politics, and current events

- awareness of a range of literary genres, their development and reception, as well as relevant critical methodologies; and understanding of the grammatical structure of modern standard French.

In addition, students completing the degree in French are expected to acquire:

- the ability to speak and understand modern, spoken standard French sufficient for all purposes of daily life and for intellectual discussion in academic settings;

- the ability to read and write modern standard French with sufficient fluency and correctness for successful literary or linguistic analysis of French texts;

- the ability to analyze and interpret literary texts in terms of style, plot, structure, characters, themes, and the use of literary devices;

- the ability to communicate such analyses and interpretations simply in French or at a more sophisticated level in English, and to discuss a wide range of topics concerning French culture, civilization, and current events; and

- the ability to follow with reasonable comprehension authentic French broadcasts or film.

(University of Colorado, Boulder, CO)

Geography

Geography aims to provide a broad-ranging perspective on humans as inhabitants and transformers of the face of the earth. The search for this understanding involves thorough study of the physical earth, its habitation by humans, and the resulting diversity of regions and places. Geographers study the physical earth by examining the interlocking systems of the natural environment including climate, landforms, soils, and biota. Humans are studied by examining those diverse historical, cultural, social, economic, and political structures and processes that affect the location and spatial organization of population groups and their activities. Regions and places, whether described as nations, cities, ecological units or landscapes, are studied by integrating and interpreting their physical and human relationships in an effort to better understand them and the problems they face.

Geographers are often found working in business, industry, government, planning and teaching. Their tasks may range from determining the optimal location for a new supermarket to doing the biophysical and socioeconomic studies required for urban and regional planning. Geographers trained in cartography may find professional opportunities in the various aspects of making and communicating with maps.

The branches of geography tend to fall into these groupings:

1) human geography—cultural, economic and urban; 2) physical geography—climatology, hydrogeography, geomorphology and biogeography; 3) regional geography—studies of regions or territories, such as East Asia, Pacific Northwest and Montana; 4) geographic concepts, methods, and techniques—historical geography, map and air photo interpretation, cartography, quantitative spatial analysis, field techniques and geographic research methods. (The University of Montana, Missoula, MT)

Geology

Geology deals with the physical and chemical nature of the Earth, the evolution and impact of life on the planet and the global processes active both now and in the past. An understanding of geology is developed through the scientific study of fossils, sedimentary, igneous and metamorphic rocks, and past and present-day ecosystems, including the oceanic realm.

Introductory courses are designed to contribute significantly to a liberal arts education and an understanding of the environment. Advanced courses provide the highest possible level of general and professional training for concentrators.

A concentration in geology provides students with the opportunity to pursue careers in the geological and environmental sciences, business and education, as well as government and public service. Upon graduation, many geology majors go on to graduate study in geology, hydrology, oceanography, environmental sciences, and environmental policy and law. Other graduates go directly into a wide spectrum of employment situations, including business, environmental consulting, teaching and administration in schools and museums, and mining and petroleum-related jobs. (Colgate University, Hamilton, NY)

Kinesiology

The curriculum offers students the opportunity to study the body of knowledge of human movement and sport, and to choose specific programs of study that allow them to pursue a particular goal related to the discipline. There is no intent to orient all students toward a particular specialized interest or occupation. This program provides a hierarchical approach to the study of human movement. First, a core of knowledge is recognized as being necessary for all students in the curriculum. These core courses are considered foundational to advanced and more specific courses. Secondly, at the "options" level, students may select from two sets of courses that they believe will provide the knowledge to pursue whatever goal they set for themselves in the future. To further strengthen specific areas of interest, students should carefully select related studies, courses and electives. (University of Maryland at College Park)

Mathematics

Mathematics is sometimes called the Queen of the Sciences; because of its unforgiving insistence on accuracy and rigor it is a model for all of science. It is a field which serves science but also stands on its own as one of the greatest edifices of human thought. Much more than a collection of calculations, it is finally a system for the analysis of form. Alone among the sciences, it is a discipline where almost every fact can and must be proved. The study of mathematics is an excellent preparation for many careers; the patterns of careful logical reasoning and analytical problem solving essential to mathematics are also applicable in contexts where quantity and measurement play only minor roles. Thus students of mathematics may go on to excel in medicine, law, politics, or business as well as any of a vast range of scientific careers. Special programs are offered for those interested in teaching mathematics at the elementary or high school level or in actuarial mathematics, the mathematics of insurance.

The other programs split between those that emphasize mathematics as an independent discipline and those that favor the application of mathematical tools to problems in other fields. There is considerable overlap here and any of these programs may serve as preparation for either further study in a variety of academic disciplines, including mathematics itself, or intellectually challenging careers in a wide variety of corporate and governmental settings. (The University of Michigan, Ann Arbor, MI)

Medical Technology

The medical technologist performs laboratory analyses on blood, tissue, and fluids in the human body using precision instruments such as microscopes and automatic analyzers. Test results play an important role in the detection, diagnosis, and treatment of disease. Medical technologists establish and monitor quality control programs and design or modify procedures to assure accurate results. They recognize interdependency of tests and understand physiological conditions affecting test results in order to provide data used by a physician in determining the presence, extent, and as far as possible, the cause of disease. (The University of Kansas, Lawrence, KS)

Music

For more than two thousand years, music has been viewed as a crucial part of education, compulsory in some cultures, optional in many, formative in all. Music is customarily regarded as an art, but as a university subject it has its own scientific language, logic, and grammar, in the understanding of which the mind is stretched and tested.

Furthermore, music as taught at Duke includes assumptions that history, theory, composition, and performance are areas of comparable worth both in themselves and as a means of understanding the many facets of musicianship. Almost every student has some personal involvement with music (often with the many kinds of music), and the courses aim to further that involvement, whether passive or active, a simple hobby or a compelling force. Courses include many kinds of instruction: applied lessons, history and theory lectures and seminars, harmony classes, composition seminars, ensemble participation, practical laboratory work (such as ear-training), coaching sessions for conductors and chamber musicians, and jazz improvisation. Emphasis is placed equally on theory and practice, and students' musical activity can vary widely across the spectrum from composing their own music to endeavoring to understand the technical, historical, and sociological context of other composers' music. (Duke University, Durham, NC)

Nursing

The Bachelor of Science in Nursing (B.S.N.) is designed to provide preparation for careers in the hospital care of patients and in community agencies such as public health services, schools, homes, and industries. It also serves as the base for graduate study in nursing.

In addition to the advantages of combining general education with specialized career preparation, a college or university program offers the advantages of full participation in the social, cultural, and recreational activities of a highly diverse campus community. In nursing, no less than in other pursuits, a college or university background enables people not only to be prepared for a career but to be able to achieve a life of thought and action informed by knowledge, introspection, and contemplation.

The program prepares professional nurses to be primary health care providers who are able to engage in a broad range of health promotion and teaching activities and to coordinate care in any sector of the health care system.

The nursing major provides a basis for nurses' roles in wellness and health promotion, in acute care, and in long-term care for chronic illness. The professional nurse provides care to individuals, families, groups, and communities along a continuum of health, illness, and disability.

In addition to providing care, the nurse serves as a coordinator of health care by organizing and facilitating the delivery of comprehensive, efficient, and appropriate service to individuals, families, groups, and communities. The nurse demonstrates the ability to conceptualize the total continuing health needs of the patient, including legal and ethical aspects of care. The program's goal is to produce graduates who are competent, committed, creative, and compassionate. (The University of Iowa, Iowa City, IA)

Occupational Therapy

Occupational therapy practice is directed toward enabling or restoring individual capacity for functional independence and adaptation in the context of clients' environments. The occupational therapy program includes studies in three major areas: 1) liberal arts; 2) biological, behavioral, and health sciences; and 3) occupational therapy theory and practice. Observation and guided practice in local clinical sites are an integral part of some courses. Following completion of the four-year academic program, students are placed in three 3-month, full-time fieldwork experiences. (University of New Hampshire, Durham, NH)

Philosophy

An education in philosophy conveys a sense of wonder about ourselves and our world. It achieves this partly through exploration of philosophical texts, which comprise some of the most stimulating creations of the human intellect, and partly through direct and personal engagement with philosophical issues. At the same time, an education in philosophy cultivates a critical stance to this elicited puzzlement, which would otherwise merely bewilder us.

The central topics of philosophy include the nature of reality (metaphysics); the ways we represent reality to ourselves and to others (philosophy of mind and philosophy of language); the nature and analysis of inference and reasoning (logic); knowledge and the ways to acquire it (epistemology and philosophy of science); and value and morality (aesthetics, ethics, and political philosophy). Students who major in philosophy are encouraged to study broadly in all of these areas of philosophy. (Amherst College, Amherst, MA)

Physics

Physics examines the fundamental principles that govern natural phenomena, ranging in scale from collisions of subatomic particles, through the behavior of solids, liquids, and biomolecules, to exploding stars and colliding galaxies.

The program aims to help students experience the

intellectual stimulation of studying physics and astro-physics and the excitement of front-line research; under-stand the basic principles and techniques of physics-related careers; and prepare for graduate study in physics or related fields.

The department offers four levels of undergraduate courses: descriptive courses for non-science majors with limited mathematical background; general survey courses for students in scientific and engineering fields; advanced courses primarily intended for physics majors; and highly advanced courses primarily intended for prospective graduate students. In addition to work in industrial, government, or high-technology laboratories in areas of applied physics, students may find opportuni-ties in such fields as biophysics, computer science, geo-physics, medical and radiation physics, and engineering. Many physics majors pursue advanced degrees in physics and related fields. (Northeastern University, Boston, MA)

Political Science

The study of governments and human beings as decision makers is at once an ancient discipline and one of the most recently developed social sciences. Political inquiry reaches back to the recorded beginnings of human society, for individuals have always been curious about the nature of governments, the bases of authority and personality of leaders, the obligations of followers, and consequences of public policies. Although interest persists in these mat-ters, inquiry has broadened to include scientific observa-tions about politics that utilize relatively new techniques of analysis that are common to many of the social sci-ences.

The newer emphasis is upon systematic procedures of investigation, rigorous standards of proof, comparative analysis and interdisciplinary studies.

Both of these approaches—the traditional and the behavioral—are offered in the undergraduate and gradu-ate levels of study. The curriculum provides background in the theory and practice of politics and techniques of methodological inquiry for the student with general inter-ests. It offers training of a general and specific nature that is useful for persons planning to seek careers in edu-cation, the legal profession, state and local government, urban and regional planning, the federal bureaucracy and journalism, or in any of the proliferating quasi-public organizations that seek to monitor the political processes or to influence the content of public policy. (Idaho State University, Pocatello, ID)

Psychology

Psychology is the scientific study of the behavior of organisms with a primary focus on human behavior. It is concerned with the biological and environmental determinants of behavior as reflected in the study of physiological, sensory, perceptual, cognitive, motivational, learning, developmental, aging and social processes. The undergraduate program seeks a balance between exposure to basic psychological principles and theories and their extension to the applied areas such as child education, counseling, mental retardation and behavioral deviancy. (University of Notre Dame, South Bend, IN)

Religious Studies

The curriculum in Religious Studies includes the study of traditions such as Buddhism, Hinduism, Taoism, Confucianism, Judaism, Islam, Christianity, and Native American and other traditional religions, and topics such as ritual studies, peace studies, religion and literature, women and religion, and religion and psychology.

Students in this curriculum are expected to gain knowledge of one major religious tradition and identify textual and artifactual data relevant to the study of religion. Central is the ability to draw connections between different historical and/or cultural contexts of religion. (University of Colorado, Boulder, CO)

Social Work

Social work assists people in the prevention and resolution of social problems. It provides services to those who seek to resolve personal difficulties and it helps communities organize services to contribute to the well-being of all citizens. It plays a significant role in the planning and administration of human service programs and the development of public policy.

Qualified social workers are in demand in every area of professional practice. For example, they are needed to work with children and adults who are mentally ill, emotionally disturbed, delinquent, physically ill, mentally or physically challenged, or economically deprived. Social work is practiced in such settings as social welfare centers, psychiatric and general hospitals, service centers for the aged, and community-based agencies of various types.

The Jane Addams College of Social Work responds to the challenges facing urban America by preparing social work practitioners, scholars, and leaders with a firm grounding in public and private sector issues facing vulnerable populations. The mission is to educate professional social workers, develop knowledge, and provide leadership in the development and implementation of policies and services on behalf of the poor, the oppressed, racial and ethnic minorities, and other at-risk urban populations. (University of Illinois at Chicago)

Sociology

Sociology covers virtually every aspect of human society: from the family and sex roles to the sociology of aging; from race and ethnic relations, education, and work, to the sociology of the environment and the study of population. Sociologists do study what are commonly regarded as social problems—crime and delinquency, drug addiction, and problems of social policy—but they also examine fundamental social processes present in any society: social change, conflict, and inequality. The central concerns of the discipline are less with practical solutions to social issues than with fundamental understandings of the workings of human society and with the explanation of social behavior.

A major in sociology can be both professional or preprofessional training and a broad liberal education. The department major provides preparation for graduate work in the social sciences and social work and skills that provide employment opportunities in the growing human and social service professions. At the same time, the core issues of sociology—problems of change and conflict in human societies—form a central part of liberal education in the contemporary world.

Although the sociology major provides an opportunity to consider systematically and objectively the nature of our society, it also provides an excellent background for a variety of occupations and careers. A concentration in social welfare and social policy can lead to employment in a federal or state government agency dealing with the administration of social services. Courses in criminology and the sociology of law are a useful preparation for a career as a probation or corrections officer or in law enforcement. Students with an interest in careers in industrial and labor relations or as personnel officers in industry should see industrial sociology and the sociology of complex organizations.

Specialization in the sociology of medicine and the sociology of mental disorders is a useful preparation for the growing health-related professions. (University of Massachusetts Amherst)

Theatre and Dance

The study of theatre and dance helps a student to understand more fully basic human qualities and to improve skills of expression, both emotively and intellectually. The department of theatre and dance is designed to accommodate a wide variety of interests. The department offers courses in the theoretical, literary, and historical concepts of theatre and in practical aspects of theatre production. All are intended to broaden the liberal education of students. For students who like to attend good theatre productions, the department provides exposure to great works from the vast catalogue of past and present drama through an extensive program in the campus theatres.

For students bent on furthering their avocational production skills, the department heartily encourages them to participate in production activities in different capacities and at various levels of expertise. In the past, nonmajors have acted, directed, designed, and both chaired and worked on every production crew, according to their desires and talents. Many opportunities are available, and credit can be earned for active participation.

Students who major in theatre fall into two broad categories. Some of them view theatre as a viable route to the personal, creative, and intellectual development needed for whatever career they choose to pursue in the future. Some seek preprofessional training for theatre careers in professional and educational theatre. Many have completed advanced graduate and conservatory work at leading institutions and have careers in theatre and in college, secondary and elementary teaching.

The art of dance is both a powerful means of self-expression and an enjoyable route to physical awareness and well-being. Within the liberal arts context, any given movement is taught within its aesthetic and historic setting. Each technique is an event that has spatial, rhythmic and dynamic implications that create and communicate a meaning between dancer and spectator. The array of courses described under dance does not constitute a major or a concentration, but is intended to allow students to explore the range of dance expression beginning at their own comfortable level. Emphasis is on both aesthetic expression and practical technique within the historical context of each. (Knox College, Galesburg, IL)

Keep on Searching

Search college catalogues for a description of the majors that interest you. Browse. Other majors may draw your attention. Compare a major in one catalogue with the same major in another one. Every school creates a major differently, combining the school's unique culture, the research of its faculty, and the academic strength of students who have studied there previously. Reading the descriptions will give you a sense of what a particular major means at each school and whether studying that particular major interests you.

Courses Required for Different Majors

Mapping out a four-year plan for all the courses you are going to take is nearly impossible. Some courses are offered every term, others only occasionally. The timetable of classes, distributed before registration every term, may bring conflicts in timing between two courses. Electives you had your heart set on may never be available when you have time. You can make a rough sketch, but that's all it is, rough.

The goal of every college student is to get the prerequisites out of the way and enjoy the electives—those courses you take by choice. A very popular elective at the University of California at San Diego, for example, is Gospel Choir, headed by Ken Anderson. He brings five hundred musically gifted and musically interested students together for hallelujahs. Music majors may also take this course as one of their required music courses.

Grinders, Weeders, and Breezes

You can learn a lot about a course from the reputation it has acquired on campus. Students may label a course a "grinder," a "weeder," or a "breeze."

Grinders

In the required courses, watch out for the "grinders." These courses, which require a lot of reading, research, memorization, and papers or impossible-to-pass tests, "grind" students down to barely recognizable apparitions of their former selves. Students in these courses move ghostlike through the campus. Almost from the first day you set foot on campus, upperclasspeople will be warning about certain courses. Taking them is the equivalent of war stories. Surviving is considered an accomplishment.

Weeders

Another category you will encounter are the "weeders." Especially prevalent in the sciences and premed curricula. These courses seem designed to "weed out" those who lack the background or stamina to meet the demands of the class. A professor will stand up the first day in organic chemistry and tell students that only half of the class will pass. "You can't all go to med school, there isn't enough room!" he will bellow to the crestfallen students. Or a creative writing instructor will so intimidate students with his or her critique of a short story that the students will drop the course before they've had a chance to understand and adapt to writing short stories.

Breezes

Some of the courses will be relatively easy, either because of your natural ability or because you were well prepared for the subject in high school. Such a course is labeled a "breeze." Consider these courses way stations along the trip, a place to catch your breath.

Prerequisites

You will quickly tire of seeing the word "prerequisite." Prerequisites, as the name implies, must be completed before you can move on to the next course. The prerequisite courses always seem to lack luster at the time you are taking them. The upper-level courses are the ones that students value for intellectual challenge. They just want to get the "prewrecks" out of the way.

The Logic of Course Sequences for Majors

College is a time of skill building. When you start out in an introductory course, you become familiar with the terrain and the vocabulary. Vocabulary is essential to communication and each specialty has its own terminology. Imagine a convention of physics majors taking place in Spokane, Washington. Within a very short period of time, no matter where the students attend school, they would be conversing in their own language. They could quickly relate and get conversationally to the problem solving that goes on in their discipline. The same is true for music majors or psych majors.

If you enroll in an Introductory Russian course, you will quickly see that the alphabet looks quite different from the Roman alphabet. Many people who have never studied Russian assume that this is the most difficult part of the course. It is not. Students must learn the alphabet during the first weekend. Until you have mastered that basic building block, there will be no progress in grammar, sentence structure, or reading great Russian authors.

Sometimes students try to skip the courses required before the one they want. Somehow, they beat the computer or the college registration process and get in without the required courses. They are at a severe disadvantage. It's similar to taking a course for which you registered late and missed the first two weeks of class. You start the class in week three. Already you feel lost. How could they have covered so much in just two short weeks, you ask. The acceleration has several reasons. The instructor is fresh and eager to impart knowledge in the first two weeks. She or he is not yet exhausted from grading papers and research. Students feel good, refreshed from an intersession break. They are especially attentive and listen carefully to every point the instructor makes. The books the class is using have already been purchased in the bookstore. The late registrants, on the other hand, find that the bookstore is out of the textbook they need and it won't be in for another two weeks. This is the same dilemma that students face who somehow take a course out of sequence. They haven't done the basic groundwork and usually feel behind.

Course sequencing follows logic and is designed to build skills. Once you have learned the basics in 100-level courses such as Human Relationships 101, you are ready to go on to upper-level courses such as Marriage in the Twentieth Century 202, Lesbian and Gay Relationships 204, etc. As you move up the ladder, you build confidence in what you have learned and apply it to the next subject under your major.

The Majors

Schools differ in what they require of their majors, but in the United States most majors involve similar studies. There are exceptions as majors continue to evolve. Many schools do not require their English majors to read Shakespeare today, including Barnard, Brown, the University of Chicago, and Princeton. A decision to not require Shakespeare makes national news, but it takes a while for a trend to be established.

To give you an idea of what you will be studying in a particular major, a sample of courses in specific majors follows. Courses vary from school to school.

Accounting

Introduction to Financial Accounting

Introduction to Managerial Accounting

Intermediate Financial Accounting

Cost Accounting

Auditing

Federal Income Tax I, II

Business Law I, II

Governmental and Nonprofit Accounting

Accounting Information Systems

International Accounting

African-American Studies

Introduction to African-American Studies

African-American Behavioral Patterns

The African-American Family in the United States

Introduction to African-American Literature I

Precolonial Africa

African-American History to 1877

Africans in Latin America and the Caribbean

African Art

Black Politics in the United States

Studies in African-American Poetry

Theory and Criticism in African-American Literature

African-Americans and the Criminal Justice System

Anthropology	Human Evolution
	Folklore
	Sex and Gender in World Cultures
	Old World Archaeology
	Culture and Personality
	The First Americans
	China and Japan: Society and Culture
	Cultural Ecology
	Geographic Information Systems
	Theory and Method in Archaeology
Architecture	Introduction to Architecture
	Structures in Design of Steel and Timber Structures
	Building Science: Multistory Residential/Office Buildings
	Design and Technology
	Architectural Study in Europe
	Architecture Design Laboratory
	Advanced Structural Analysis
	Computers in Architecture
	Theory of Architecture and Building Analysis
	Professional Practice
Art and Design	Drawing I, II
	Graphic Design I, II, III, IV, V, VI, VII, VIII
	Industrial Design, I, II
	Sculpture I, II
	Photography, I, II
	Introduction to Time-Based Visual Arts
	Introduction to Computer Graphics
	Color Theory
	Typography
	Painting I, II
	Lithography
	Relief Printmaking

Media Explorations

Cinema I, II

Video I, II

Art Education

Computer-Aided Design

Advanced Film/Video/Animation

Electronic Visualization

Art Therapy

Art History

Introduction to Art and Art History

History of Art and Architecture I, II

Theories and Methods in the History of Art and
Architecture

History of Landscape Architecture

Twentieth Century Architecture

History of Photography I, II

History of Film I, II

History of Design I, II

Art and Architecture of the Ancient World I, II

American Art to 1945

Contemporary Architecture

Biochemistry

Introductory Physics I, II

Biology of Cells and Organisms

Biology of Populations and Communities

Mendelian and Molecular Genetics

General and Analytical Chemistry I, II

Organic Chemistry I, II

Organic Chemistry Laboratory

Physical Chemistry I, II

Physical Chemistry Laboratory

Biochemistry I, II

Intermediate Inorganic Chemistry

Bioengineering	Introduction to Bioengineering
	Senior Design I, II
	Pattern Recognition
	Biomechanics
	Fields and Waves in Biological Materials
	Biological Signal Analysis
	Real-Time Data Processing
	Digital Signal Processing
Biology	Biology of Cells and Organisms
	Biology of Populations and Communities
	Mendelian and Molecular Genetics and Laboratory
	Writing in the Biological Sciences
	Cell Biology and Laboratory
	Vertebrate Embryology
	General Microbiology and Laboratory
	Developmental Biology and Laboratory
	Cell and Molecular Biology
	Ultrastructural Cell Biology
	Plant Growth and Development and Laboratory
	Biochemistry I, II
Chemical Engineering	Introduction to Thermodynamics
	Material and Energy Balances
	Chemical Engineering: Thermodynamics
	Transport Phenomena I, II, III
	Chemical Reaction Engineering
	Chemical Process Control
	Chemical Engineering Laboratory I, II
	Senior Design I, II
	Properties of Materials
	Fortran Programming for Engineers
	Electrical Circuit Analysis

Chemistry	General College Chemistry I, II
	Organic Chemistry I and Laboratory
	Organic Chemistry II and Laboratory
	Physical Chemistry I and Laboratory
	Physical Chemistry II and Laboratory
	Inorganic Chemistry I
	Introductory Biochemistry
	Analytical Chemistry
Civil Engineering	Statics
	Strength of Materials
	Structural Analysis
	Hydraulics and Hydrology
	Environmental Pollution Control
	Properties of Materials
	Composition and Properties of Concrete
	Behavior and Design of Metal Structures
	Introduction to Transportation and Traffic Engineering
	Design of Reinforced Concrete Structures
	Soil Mechanics and Foundation Engineering
	Senior Design I, II
	Finite Element Analysis I
	Fortran Programming for Engineers
	Electrical Circuit Analysis
Communication	Effective Public Communication
	Communication and Culture
	Interpersonal Communication
	Media Processes and Effects
	Communication Technologies
	Communication Analysis
	Communication in the Corporate Setting
	Group Communication
	Communication Research

Organizational Communication Media Field Production

Writing for the Print Media

Professional Speech Writing

Public Opinion and Public Communication

Criminal Justice

Introduction to the Justice System

Law in Society

Principles of Criminal Law

Criminology

Criminal Justice Organizations

Research Methods I, II

Introduction to the Criminal Courts

Senior Studies in Criminal Justice

Juvenile Justice System

Organized White Collar Crime in the United States

Economics

Macroeconomics in the World Economy: Theory and Applications

Managerial Economics

Business Conditions Analysis

Comparative Economic Systems

Government and Business

History of Economic Thought

Introduction to Mathematical Economics

Econometrics

Electrical Engineering and Computer Science

Statistics and Dynamics

Thermodynamics

Engineering Economy

Fortran Programming for Engineers

Electrical Circuit Analysis

Digital Systems

Circuits and Signal Processing

Communication Engineering

Transmission Lines

Electromagnetic Fields

Electronic Devices and Circuits

Electronic Circuit Design

Computer Organization and Programming

Senior Design I, II

Elementary Education

Policy Foundations

The Educative Process

Literacy and Elementary Education

Introductory Fieldwork in Elementary Education

Reading and Writing Through the Elementary Grades

Teaching Elementary School Mathematics and Science

Teaching and Learning for Children of Various Abilities and Cultures

Social Studies and Literature in Elementary Education

Student Teaching in the Elementary Grades

Survey of Characteristics of Exceptional Children

English

Understanding Literature

American Literature and Culture

Introduction to Literary Criticism

History of English Literature I: Beginnings to 1700

History of English Literature II: 1700 to 1900

Topics in Literature: 1900 to the Present

Introduction to Nonfiction Writing

Advanced Nonfiction Writing

Introduction to Fiction or Poetry Writing

Advanced Fiction or Poetry Writing

Writing for the Print Media

Finance

Personal Finance

Introduction to Managerial Finance

Investments

Managerial Finance

Portfolio Management

Security Analysis

Options and Futures Markets

Corporate Financial Strategy

Introduction to Money and Banking

International Finance

Small Business Finance

Geology

Principles of Physical Geology

Principles of Historical Geology

Mineralogy

Topics in Modern Geology

Introduction to Petrology

Principles of Sedimentology and Stratigraphy

Introduction to Paleontology

Field Geology

Structural Geology and Tectonics

Health Information Management

Introduction to the Health Care System

Medical Science I, II

Health Information Management I, II, III

Technical Affiliation

Legal Aspects of Medical Records

Coding and Classification Systems I, II

Analysis of Health Care Data

Quality Evaluation and Management

Management I, II

Computers in Health Care

Systems Analysis

Introduction to Research

Health Information Research

Current Issues in Health Information Management

Financial Management

Clinical Practicum

History

Western Civilization to 1648

Western Civilization Since 1648

American Civilization to the Late Nineteenth Century

American Civilization Since the Late Nineteenth Century

World History

Europe: 1815 to 1914

China Since 1911

Latin America Since 1850

The Middle East Since 1258

Military History: War Since Napoleon

Senior Seminar: Topics in Research and Writing

Teaching History and the Related Disciplines

Topics in African History

Topics in Revolutionary and Early National United States History

Human Nutrition and Dietetics

Foods

Nutrition

Nutrition Care Planning

Instructional Design

Management

Science of Foods

Food and its Facets

Science and Nutrition

Nutrition Through the Life Cycle

Nutrition Through the Life Cycle Practicum

Clinical Nutrition I, II, III

Clinical Practice I, II, III

Quantity Food Production

Quantity Food Production Practicum

Food Service Management

Food Service Management Practicum

Seminar

The Research Process

Management in Human Nutrition and Medical Dietetics

Professional Practice

Fundamentals of Biochemistry

Principles of Delivering Public Health Nutrition Services

Human Physiology

Information and Decision Sciences

Business Computing I

Business Systems Simulation

Business Statistics

Quality and Productivity Improvement Using Statistical Methods

Management Information Systems

Computer Performance Evaluation and Modeling

Operations Management

Operations Research

Italian

Conversational Italian

Italian Composition and Conversation

Introduction to Reading and Analysis of Italian Literary Texts

Advanced Italian Composition and Conversation

Advanced Italian Grammar

Modern Italian Literature and Society

Literary Forms in Early Renaissance

Writing and Research in the Major

Contemporary Italian Literature

Divina Commedia I

Italian Phonetics

Italian Culture and Civilization

History of the Italian Language

Kinesiology	Biology of Cells and Organisms
	Introduction to Psychology
	English Composition I, II
	Interpersonal Communication
	Introduction to the Kinesiology Profession
	Fundamental Movement Skills
	Human Physiological Anatomy I, II
	Philosophical and Psychosocial Aspects of Movement
	Functional Anatomy
	Physiology of Exercise
	Perceptual-Motor Learning and Development
	Evaluation in Physical Education and Health
Latin American Studies	Introduction to Latin America in a World Context
	Introduction to Contemporary Latin America
	Expository Writing on Latin American Topics
	Latin America Since 1850
	Mexico Since 1850
	History of Modern Puerto Rico
	Central American Culture and Literary Studies
	Topics in Latino Community Studies
	Problems of South American Ethnology
	Latinas in the United States
Management	Organizational Analysis and Practice
	Organizational Behavior
	Human Resource Management
	Labor-Management Relations
	Negotiation and Conflict Resolution
	Compensation and Reward Systems
	Career Planning and Development
	Managerial Effectiveness Through Diversity
	Impact of Technological Change
	Industrial Sociology

Marketing	Consumer Market Behavior
	Marketing Research and Information Systems
	Marketing Management
	Principles of Retailing
	Small Business Consulting
	The Personal Selling Effort in Marketing
	Advertising and Sales Promotion
	Product Management
	Comparative Marketing Systems
Mathematics	Calculus for Mathematics, Engineering, and Science I, II, III
	Writing for Mathematics
	Linear Algebra
	Abstract Algebra
	Advanced Calculus I, II
	Complex Analysis with Applications
	Formal Logic
Mechanical Engineering	Statistics
	Strength of Materials
	Fortran Programming for Engineers
	Electrical Circuit Analysis
	Engineering Economy
	Engineering Graphics and Design
	Thermodynamics
	Dynamics of Rigid Bodies
	Fluid Mechanics I, II
	Technical Vibrations
	Mechanisms and Dynamics of Machinery
	Heat Transfer
	Experimental Methods in ME
	Manufacturing Process Principles
	Senior Design
	Introduction to Computer-Aided Design

Music	Music Theory I, II, III, IV
	Ear Training I, II, III, IV
	Keyboard Skills I, II, III, IV
	Music History I, II, III
	Counterpoint
	Analytic Techniques
	Jazz
	Opera
	Music for Symphony Orchestra
	Composition
	Conducting
	Convocation/Recital
	Concert Band
	University Choir
	Early Music Consort
	Jazz Ensemble
Occupational Therapy	Human Physiological Anatomy I, II
	Introduction to Psychology
	Statistics in Psychology
	Abnormal Psychology
	Developmental Psychology
	Classical Etymology in the Life Sciences
	Occupational Therapy Fundamentals
	Neurological Foundations of Occupational Performance I
	Development of Occupational Performance I, II
	Sociocultural Aspects of Occupational Therapy
	Biomechanical Interventions I, II
	Neurological Interventions with Children
	Psychosocial Intervention I, II
	Occupational Therapy Processes
	Organizational Systems for Practice
	Neurological Interventions with Adults
	Research in Occupational Therapy

Philosophy	Introduction to Philosophy
	Introductory Logic
	Symbolic Logic
	Ancient Philosophy I: Plato and His Predecessors
	History of Modern Philosophy I: Descartes and His Successors
	Medieval Philosophy
	The Philosophy of Psychology
	Metaphysics
	Topics in Ethics and Political Philosophy
	Morality and the Law
	The Philosophy of Death
	Understanding Art
Physical Therapy	Human Physiological Anatomy I
	Introduction to Psychology
	Statistics in Psychology
	Neuroanatomy for Allied Health Professions
	Gross Human Anatomy I, II
	Physiology and Biophysics
	Introduction to Physical Therapy
	Communication, Education, and the Profession
	Kinesiology
	Therapeutic Exercise I, II
	Physical Agents
	Clinical Neurology
	Orthopaedics
	Clinical Lectures in Psychiatry and Pediatrics
	Clinical Instruction and Practice I, II, III
	Community Resources for Health Care
	Management
	Critical Inquiry in Physical Therapy
	Orthopaedic Physical Therapy
	Rehabilitation I, II
	Culture and Rehabilitation
	Pathophysiology

Physics	General Physics I, II, III, IV
	Electromagnetism I
	Quantum Mechanics I
	Theoretical Mechanics I
	Thermal and Statistical Physics
	Mathematical Methods for Physicists
	Modern Experimental Physics I
Political Science	Introduction to American Government and Politics
	Introduction to Political Analysis I, II
	American Political Theories
	Introduction to International Relations
	Topics in Comparative Politics
	State Government
	The Mass Media and Politics
	Topics in Political Behavior
	Possible Political Systems: Ideal and Actual
Psychology	Introduction to Psychology
	Research in Psychology
	Writing in Psychology
	Statistical Methods in Behavioral Science
	Cognition and Memory
	Abnormal Psychology
	Social Psychology
	Theories of Personality
	Learning
	Developmental Psychology
Russian	Russian Composition and Conversation I, II, III, IV
	Introduction to Russian Literature I, II
	Writing About Literature
	Structure of Modern Russian
	Studies in the Russian Novel

Studies in Russian Literature

Dostoyevsky

Women in Russian Literature

Social Work
Introduction to Practice Skills

Practice I, II

Human Behavior and the Social Environment

Human Service Organizations in the Community

Majority and Minority Cultural Interaction

Social Welfare Policy and Services

Social Work Research

Field Instruction I, II

Integrative Seminar

Family Theory and Practice

Group Theory and Practice

Community Theory and Practice

Sociology
Introduction to Sociology

Introductory Sociological Statistics

Introduction to Sociological Research

Sociological Analysis

Explaining Social Life

Social Inequalities

Youth and Society

Gender and Society

African-Americans and the Criminal Justice System

Industrial Society

Theater
Introduction to Theater

Theater Production

Fundamentals of Acting

Script Analysis

Design for the Stage

Drama in Its Cultural Context I, II

Stage Direction

Characterization

Advanced Acting: Classical Greek Through
     Shakespeare

Practicum in Acting

Modern American Theater

Asian Theater Traditions

Scene and Lighting Design

The Actor's Voice

Costume and Makeup Design

Audition Technique

Stage Direction

If the courses in any of these majors seem interesting to
you, that major should be investigated further. Perhaps
you have never considered a degree in health information
management or realized what a major in music involves.
Majors differ from school to school depending on the faculty. The catalogues of the schools you are considering will
list the courses required in a major and provide descriptions. Shop and compare what a major means at each
school.

The New, Unusual, and Design-Your-Own Majors

Some majors weren't around when your parents went to school—women's studies, urban planning, sports management. They have evolved because society evolves. The new majors may be a response to areas that have become marketable and are tied to the prospect of jobs. Others, such as the study of gender, result from philosophical evolution. Many are interdisciplinary, which means you attend classes in several different departments and broaden your understanding of a field.

New Majors   A description of some of the new majors follows. You won't find them on every campus. Then, of course, there is the option of designing your own major, an alternative offered at some schools. Perhaps you will find something here you did not know existed. At the very least, it should

125

make you aware of a wide range of choices. Inquire whether your area of interest is available in a new major at the school you are attending or planning to attend.

Toy Design

Just because you're going to college doesn't mean you have to give up your Legos, Etch-A-Sketch, or Cabbage Patch dolls. Bring them along as icons of design inspiration while at the Fashion Institute of Technology in New York City. Students may study a number of design majors including toys, advertising, fabric, fashion, illustration, interiors, packaging, apparel, and others. If you opt for toys, your curriculum will include Marker Rendering, Soft Toy and Doll Design, Motor Learning, Hard Toys, Computer Technology, Probability and Geometry, Toy Business Practices, and Toy Advertising and Promotion. Perhaps you will design the next Tickle Me Elmo.

Women and Gender Studies

The forces that shape the position of women and men in our society were not subjects of widespread study until the late 1960s, when faculty and students began to conduct new research. Eleanor Roosevelt and Jane Addams were popular historical figures, but little research had been done on how societal forces had affected them or other women. The realities of gender had not been documented. The interest in these subjects was widespread and gradually colleges began to offer majors in women's studies. Today, 250 colleges and universities offer a women's studies major and 111 offer graduate programs.

A cornerstone of this major is feminist theory, the study of the complex intersections of gender with every part of civilization and culture. The introductory women's studies course at Wesleyan College in Middletown, Connecticut, for instance, describes the study this way:

> . . . introduces students to major issues and approaches in women's studies through selected works in the social sciences, humanities, and natural sciences. Modes of understanding women's nature, sexuality, personal relationships, and public roles, as well as the ways in which the study of gender has changed traditional scholarship, are examined. An emphasis on the experience of minority women is maintained in the course.

A sample of courses you might take in women's studies are:

Daytime Serials: Family and Social Roles

Childbirth in the United States

The Economics of the Family

Thinking Queer

A History of Women's Voices in America

Psychology of Women

Sociology of Gender and the Military

Women and Violence

Seminar on Rape Education and Awareness

Women Writers

Poetry by Women

Women of Color

Toni Morrison

Social Change in Latin America

Seminar on Eating Disorders

Power and Poverty in the Postindustrial City

Foreign Study

Women and Religion

Women and Poverty

Women and Technology

Women and the Law

Ecofeminism

A course offered at Harvard University in Boston, "Women's Studies 123: Gender and the Professionalization of Health Care in the United States," is described in the catalogue as follows:

> The terms "man midwife" and "lady doctor" suggest the importance of gender in the history of American medicine. In fiction and art as well as in public argument, 19th- and 20th-century Americans puzzled over the decline of the "village healer," the rise and fall of women's medical school, and the professional-

ization of nursing. In the rural south as well as the urban north, notions of race and class intersected with ideas about what was appropriate work for women. This seminar will explore these transformations through recent scholarship in women's history through a sampling of period sources.

Many colleges offer women's studies as an interdisciplinary minor rather than a major. Northeastern University in Boston describes its program as follows:

> The Women's Studies program offers students an opportunity to work with respected scholars in a variety of disciplines to examine the human experience through the perspectives of women. This interdisciplinary program examines the importance of gender in societies around the world, past and present. The curriculum encourages students to learn and think about how changing beliefs about women and men have affected research and scholarship in the arts, humanities, and social and natural sciences. Students learn about gender stereotypes, the various ways ideas about gender roles and sexuality have developed, and the changing situation for women and men today.
>
> Key questions are posed that change how people see the world: How does gender influence the kinds of questions we can ask of the world around us? What information can become data when you use gender as a central part of examining a problem?

The University of Chicago, which resisted women's studies for many years, recently opened its Center for Gender Studies. Several schools, including Stanford, and the Universities of Missouri, Michigan, and Illinois at Chicago have changed the names of their Center for the Study of Women to Center for the Study of Women and Gender.

Studying gender, the social and cultural expression of sex, is designed to enrich your awareness and inform your judgments. Not incidentally, it will save you from incorrectly calling adult women "girls" or "ladies," or calling adult men "boys" or "gentlemen."

Urban Studies
The evolution of the city affects life in the city as well as in the suburbs, the state, and the nation. Transportation, energy sources, environment, pollution, class structure, crime, education, politics all provide material and vantage points for urban studies. Sometimes called "urban and regional planning," this course of study prepares students for work in government and the private sector. Frequently, the major is interdisciplinary and courses are offered in architecture, engineering, sociology, environmental studies and history. Courses you might take in this major are:

> History of the American City
>
> Planning and Environmental Values
>
> Downtown Planning
>
> Introduction to Housing Policy
>
> Community and Neighborhood Revitalization
>
> Land Use Techniques
>
> Urban Mass Transportation
>
> Introduction to Housing Markets
>
> Economics of Poverty
>
> Urban Geography
>
> Urban Anthropology

The University of Connecticut uses this description of the major:

> In general, the focus of the courses is on the development of metropolitan areas and on urban based phenomena. The intent of the program is to ensure the student a broad perspective on cities by exposure to a variety of approaches to their study as illustrated by courses drawn from Anthropology, Economics, Geography, History, Political Science and Sociology. In addition, students majoring in these disciplines may find work in Urban Studies an appropriate related group to complete their field of concentration requirement. The range of choice open to students is considerable and permits students to construct a plan of study with any of a variety of emphases.

Sports Management

As America has progressed heavily into health issues and physical fitness, the field of sports management has mushroomed. At Ferris State University in Big Rapids, Michigan, students can major in Golf or Tennis Management. Since these programs were started in the mid-80s, the placement rate has been 100 percent with graduates taking jobs as teaching professionals, directors at clubs, club managers, camp directors, pro shop managers, manufacturer sales reps, and industry administrators. Approximately 45 percent of the degree is in business, 30 percent is in general studies, and 25 percent is specific to sport management. Approximately 25 to 50 students enroll in one of these programs each year. After graduation they work in exotic places as teaching pros with a starting salary of $30,000.

"You don't have to be a great tennis player, but most of our students have played competitively," said Scott Schultz, director of the program in tennis. "Some prospective students overestimate how good they have to be. At country clubs and resorts there are plenty of beginners and intermediates who need lessons," he said, citing resorts in Spain, Germany, and Hawaii where recent graduates have found jobs. "And tell students there are many opportunities for women," Schultz added.

Environmental Studies

As concern for the environment has become foremost, schools have responded by offering an interdisciplinary major on the subject. One of the schools that offers this new major is the United States International University with campuses in San Diego, Mexico City, and Nairobi. The environmental studies major at the San Diego campus offers an overview of environmental science and how people shape and experience the world. The major focuses on the "different biotic and abiotic components of the environment as well as sustainable resource management, pollution, endangered species, population and the challenge of limited resources." The course of study offers courses in environmental ethics, economics and the law with emphasis on developing solutions by working with people.

Multilingual Journalism

Another interdisciplinary program, the multilingual journalism degree program at Lehman College, The City University of New York, brings together the departments of Languages and Literature, Art, English, Speech and

Theatre, and Black Studies. Students involved in this program must take 12 credits of advanced foreign language courses, 9 credits of Print Media, 9 credits of Electronic Media and 12 credits of Multilingual Journalism. Students graduating with this degree are prepared to cover ethnic areas of the United States or to report on events in foreign countries.

Among the courses offered in this major are:

The Italian-American Community

Anthropological Linguistics

Inequality in Cross-Cultural Perspectives

Afro-Caribbean Heritage

Black Women in American Society

Migration and the Puerto Rican Community in the U.S.

The Economy of Puerto Rico

Television Directing

Broadcast Programming

American Jewish History

The Mainland Borough: The Bronx as a City in History

Human Ecology

College of the Atlantic in Bar Harbor, Maine, only has one major: human ecology. Don't come if you want to pursue a major in any other subject.

Besides the 36 credit hours in subjects pertaining to human ecology, students must complete a community service experience, a contribution of time and energy to building and supporting the college or island community, and write a human ecology essay, which describes the student's development as a human ecologist and demonstrates competence in writing.

In addition to a freshman year advisor, students are expected to develop other relationships with faculty in order to develop significant courses of study. By senior year students are expected to work closely with a two- or three-person team in readiness for graduation. Members of the team may be other students or members of the COA community. Flexibility is honored. If one advisor doesn't fit, students are urged to seek out another and to consult faculty frequently as questions arise and decisions must be made.

The curriculum is organized into three resource areas: arts and design, environmental science, and human studies. Two courses from each of the resource areas is required, each by a different instructor.

Among the course listings are:

Conservation of Endangered Species

Functional Vertebrate Anatomy

Animal Behavior Computer Assisted Data Analysis

Electronic Photography Studio

Politics and Communication: The Mexican Mass Media as an Ecosystem

The Eye and the Poet

Understanding Culture Through Photography

Culture of Maine Woodworkers

Cultural Ecology of Population Control Practices

Contemporary Psychology: Development of Ecological Perspective

Modern Architecture: Survey of 19th and 20th Centuries

The Aesthetics of Violence

History of Western Music

Nature, People and Property: An Introduction to Political Economy

Women/Men in Transition

Weed Ecology

Agroecology

Environmental Journalism

Leadership Studies

Abraham Lincoln learned how to be a leader studying in a log cabin, but today colleges are offering a major to help students learn the skills. Apparently, there is a dearth of leadership in the world, with few people ready to step into the shoes of Winston Churchill, Mother Theresa, or Martin Luther King Jr. Approximately forty colleges offer leadership courses or training.

A $20 million gift from Robert Jepson, an alum, allowed the University of Richmond in Virginia to found the Jepson School of Leadership Studies in 1992. The definition of leadership at this school is "service, not power or glory." Among the subjects that students take are decision making, motivation, conflict resolution communication, and leading change.

At Alverno College in Milwaukee the major is called Community Leadership and Development. It meets in Alverno's Weekend College, every other weekend. The curriculum is designed to:

- Creatively address social problems with effective management skills
- Conduct financial analyses and social scientific research to reach solutions
- Explore the moral and ethical dimensions of community issues
- Draw on diverse political and cultural perspectives to develop your own philosophy
- Evaluate the effectiveness of different approaches to solving community needs

Food Service and Management

People with knowledge of food service and business run restaurants, hotels, and clubs. At the New England Culinary Institute in Montpelier, Vermont, students learn these skills while earning the B.A. in service and management. Before enrolling, students must be good cooks. They may have earned an associate's degree at the school in culinary arts or worked in the industry and earned an associate's degree at another school.

More than 70 percent of the student's time is spent managing the Institute's restaurants, bakeshops, cafeterias, and catering and banquet operations. Three other courses are required. According to the catalogue:

> The first of these focuses on the underlying skills essential to all adults: the ability to think creatively and critically, to identify problems, to do research as necessary, and to organize perceptions into a point of view that can be communicated in writing and in speaking. The second course will involve a practical study of Spanish with the goal of serving customers and managing employees using that language. Spanish was chosen since it is the

second most widely used language in American kitchens.

The final course is a class in personal/professional development. This class will explore service as a way of taking care of oneself and others. It will include work in self-assessment, group process/management styles, team building, and conflict resolution.

Therapeutic Riding

A positive interaction between disabled people and horses is the focus of the therapeutic riding major. Through this relationship specialists in this field help promote the healing process. One of the first barrier-free campuses, St. Andrews College in Laurinburg, N.C., has the first and only therapeutic riding major in the United States. A church-related institution, St. Andrews is committed to accommodating students with physical challenges. The therapeutic riding major provides career training for the disabled, as well as the able-bodied student. Students learn how to manage and understand horses, develop their skills as riders, understand the theory of riding instruction, communicate orally and in written form, understand the safety, medical management, and ethical issues necessary in this field, and develop their knowledge of the various disabling conditions and the practical applications of horseback riding as a therapeutic modality.

With a Therapeutic Riding Business Management degree, graduates can become a therapeutic riding facility manager, program manager or operator, therapeutic operations manager, or development officer.

Peace Studies

As a response to issues in the escalating arms race and the war in Vietnam, Colgate University formed the Peace Studies Program in 1970. According to the school's catalogue,

the purpose of the program is to develop a rigorous and intellectually responsible approach to the issues of war and peace, conflict and social change, violence and nonviolence. The program uses the specialized research in the interdisciplinary field of peace studies as well as relevant work in the traditional social sciences and other disciplines to understand the obstacles to world peace and possible solutions. It also explores direct, practical approaches to confronting the real conflict situations that threaten peace.

With a degree in peace studies students may work in international agencies and nongovernmental organizations concerned with human rights and conflict resolution. As the catalogue states, "Work for such agencies is often integrated with professional careers in law, journalism, the ministry, the media, education and community organizing. With an advanced degree, this major may be used in teaching peace studies at colleges and universities." Courses in this major include:

Movements for Peace and Social Change

Conflict Resolution and Mediation

Women and Peace: War, Resistance and Justice

Images of War and Peace in Twentieth-Century Art, Literature and Film

Peace and War: The European Experience

Long Island University, in its Friends World Program at Southampton, New York, offers a major called Peace Studies, Conflict Resolution and Social Change. Its catalogue cites a quotation from Margaret Mead: "Never doubt that a small group of thoughtful, committed citizens can change the world. Indeed, it's the only thing that ever has."

The program emphasizes that merely a desire to bring about positive change without the necessary education can actually worsen the situation in Third World countries. To empower its students the program focuses on recognizing the source of conflict, developing strategies for its resolution, and recognizing the complexities of conflict resolution.

Students spend their first year in the United States studying the subject of conflict and in their second year proceed to either the Middle East or Europe to study their academic interests while also taking part in field projects in areas of conflict resolution.

Cognitive Science and Cultural Studies

Faculty concerned with the nature of representation offer courses in the Cognitive Science and Cultural Studies School at Hampshire College in Amherst, Massachusetts. Cognitive scientists research how knowledge and information are represented and used by minds and brains, human or animal; and by machines, such as computers. Faculty in cultural studies are concerned with the ways in which cultural systems and cultural products represent and shape human experience and social life.

The college states that its program of Cognitive Science is the first of its kind in the country and that Cultural Studies reflect an intellectual movement that is gaining momentum nationally and internationally. Faculties of both disciplines are studying computers with an eye to the role they play in contemporary life, eager to witness contributions they can make to intellectual and artistic activity. The contribution of artificial intelligence and the new information age are of special interest in this curriculum.

Courses range from Twentieth-Century Continental Philosophy to The Psychology of the Human-Computer Interface.

Emergency Administration and Planning

Disasters happen. But now, people with a major in emergency administration and planning are ready and able to deal with these inevitabilities. The University of North Texas in Denton, Texas, claims to be the only university in the United States to offer such an undergraduate degree. According to one of the school's bulletins: "Emergency administration is a 'people' field. While majoring in emergency administration and planning, you will become skilled in interpersonal communication, leadership and planning. You will learn about the use of computers in emergency management. You may study city and state governments through courses in political science and public administration, or you may choose to study business administration." The faculty consists of individuals who have extensive practical experience as disaster planners for the military and the Red Cross or as disaster researchers. As with so many of the newer majors, this one, too, is an interdisciplinary degree.

Multicultural Studies

Many campuses offer a major or a program in multicultural studies. Based on the reality that America is a land of many people, each with ethnic diversity and talents to contribute, this major seeks to inform the student of history, language, and civilizations of different cultures. At Union College in Schenectady, New York, the program is called Multidisciplinary Studies and offers two concentrations: Africana Studies and American Studies.

Africana Studies offers an interdepartmental major in the systematic study of the history, culture, intellectual heritage, and social development of Africa and people of African descent, the societies of which they are a part, and their interactions within world civilization, according to the school's catalogue. In geography, the program covers the Atlantic world of cultural interaction including the United States, the Caribbean, Latin America, the African continent, and European areas where interaction or contact exists.

American Studies is another program offered at Union and other colleges that focuses on the study of all aspects of the United States. As the catalogue describes it:

> Students selecting this major will be expected to choose their courses from various disciplines and develop an appropriate level of mastery in one. They will work closely with an advisor to work out a thematic core around which to build their course of study. The core can be broadly defined in categories such as culture, social analysis, and politics, or more narrowly defined in areas in which a sufficient number of courses are offered. Among the latter are business enterprise, African-American or minority studies, the global impact of the United States and others.

A similar emphasis is the focus at Skidmore College in Saratoga Springs, New York, and other schools where American Studies is an interdisciplinary major with guidance in courses provided by an advisor.

Among the courses offered at Skidmore are:

Introduction to American Culture: Pre–Civil War and Post–Civil War

American Identities: Pre-1870s and post-1870s

Regional Culture: The Hudson River, the West, the South, New England

Response to War

Ethnic and Immigrant Experience

Women and Work in America

American Autobiography

Topics in American Culture: War, City, America on the Couch, Religion, Disorderly Women (An examination of women characterized by the larger society as unruly, disruptive, radical, militant, unfeminine—just generally disorderly—and what this characterization reveals about American society.)

World Hunger

World Hunger is a major at Kenyon College in Gambier, Ohio, through its program called Synoptic Majors. This major is for students whose interests lie between or among departments and allows them to combine a study of two or more subjects. World Hunger combines biology, economics, and sociology. Other recent synoptic majors have combined courses in biology and chemistry (with the emphasis on how the brain works), and psychology to form Behavioral Psychology; and courses in classics, history, and religion to form Middle East Studies.

Turfgrass Management

Under the category of Crop and Soil Sciences, students at Michigan State University in East Lansing, Michigan, may major in Turfgrass Management. In this major students study urban agriculture. The knowledge of the biological and physical sciences has expanded and improved the use of land. At the same time scientists have found ways to increase plant adaptation to environmental and other stresses. As a result, graduates of this program find jobs in industries involved with management of lawns, athletic fields, golf courses, and park and ground maintenance. In pursuing this major students take courses in plant biology, chemistry, plant genetics, management of turfgrass pests, soil fertility, entomology, and principles of weed science, to name a few.

Aeronautical Science

The Wright Brothers' flight in 1903 stirred imaginations and the desire for aeronautical education. The Embry-Riddle School of Aviation was formed in 1926 in Cincinnati. Three years later, the school became a subsidiary of AVCO, the parent of American Airlines. In the 1930s the Great Depression kept the school dormant, only to become a needed source of education for pilots and mechanics during the second World War.

Today, the locations at Daytona Beach and at a second campus in Prescott, Arizona, offer many mild-weather days to gain flying experience. The school's promotional motto is "There is one university—one—where everyone aims at the stars." Among the majors offered are aviation business administration, professional aeronautics, aerospace engineering, civil engineering, engineering physics, aviation computer science, aerospace studies, aeronautical science, and aviation maintenance management.

Subsonic and supersonic wind tunnels and a smoke tunnel on campus enable the student to simulate flying experiences. Flight instruction is given in a fleet of three single-engine Cessna 172 trainers, 26 Aerospatiale Tampico TB-9s, 5 twin-engine Cessnas, and a Beech Ing Air C90A. Single-engine and multiengine simulators, a weather room, and dispatch headquarters are also on campus, which is on the boundary of the Daytona Beach International Airport.

Bachelor of Arts in Engineering

Usually an engineering major has to sacrifice the benefits of a liberal arts education in order to complete all the required courses in his or her specialty. Not at Lafayette College in Easton, Pennsylvania, where the two disciplines have been combined in an innovative program. Called the A.B. in Engineering, the degree does not prepare students to practice as engineers but rather for careers in law, architecture, public policy, medicine, technical sales, technical writing, project construction, information systems, and environmental management fields in which a technical background is a recognized asset.

The difference between an A.B. degree and a B.S. degree is broken down at the college as:

	A.B.	B.S.
Mathematics and Physical Science	8 courses	8 courses
Technical	13 courses	26 courses
Humanities and Social Science	16 courses	9 courses

According to the catalogue, the Bachelor of Arts in Engineering degree blends a background of math and science with an understanding of human behavior and a sensitivity to the human condition through courses in history, literature, language and philosophy, psychology, sociology, and political science.

Residential Property Management

In response to industry demand for more and better-trained professionals in the housing industry, a residential property management major was established in 1985 by Virginia Tech, in Blacksburg, Virginia. So strong was the industry's commitment that more than $200,000 has been donated by industry professionals to support the program. Besides courses in the humanities, the degree requires 45 credits in property management, including Family Housing, Maintenance for Property Managers, Barrier-Free Design, Survey of Accounting, Contemporary Issues in Property Management, and Marketing Management. In elective courses students may take Real Estate Law, Issues in Aging, Organization Behavior, and Public Speaking. Local property management firms provide paid internships to access extra help during busy times of the year and to review a potential pool of future employees. Graduates manage income-producing properties such as apartment communities, shopping centers, and office buildings. Because Virginia Tech has the only RPM program in the country, students are in great demand when they graduate, according to Dr. Rosemary Goss, Professor of Housing.

Hawaiian Studies

You may not realize that you can actually study a major in Hawaii. Since many people believe that it doesn't matter what you major in, as long as you develop skills critical to life success, why not study an island in the Pacific? This major, offered at the University of Hawai'i at Manoa, will expose you to Hawaiian Genealogies, Chiefs of Post-Contact Hawai'i, Myths of Hawaiian History, and Pana O'ahu: Famous Place Names. The last is a survey of the famous place names in each 'ahupua'a of O'ahu, including accounts of mythical heroes, heiau, fishponds, wind, rain names, and their metaphoric value in Hawaiian literature.

Sport Sciences

Every sport is big business today and getting into any of these popular fields requires preparation. At Ohio University in Athens, the Sports Sciences major offers a choice of six specializations: Aquatic Management, Coaching, Exercise Physiology, Sport Industry, Sport for Special Populations, and Youth Sports. Aquatic Management courses include CPR, Coaching Sports for the Disabled, Synchronized Swimming, Diving and Competitive Swimming, Cultural Anthropology, and Psychology of Personality.

Graduates with a major in Sport Sciences lead programs at every educational level, manage recreational facilities and clubs, and coach serious athletes.

Bagpiping   One of the reasons Carnegie Mellon University in Pittsburgh gives for its major in bagpiping is that no opportunities existed anywhere in the world for the serious student of bagpipes to get conservatory training. Students of voice, jazz, keyboard, and band instruments have ample opportunities at many campuses.

Then there was the fact that Andrew Carnegie, the founder of the university, had a rich Scottish tradition and was rich. A famous bagpiper, James McIntosh, had moved his bagpiping business from Maryland to be director of the pipe band. He had taught extensively in Australia, France, Scotland, Canada and the United States, and is a well-known authority on the classical music of the bagpipe, piobaireachd. So Carnegie Mellon became the first conservatory in the world to offer a complete classical program of music study leading to a Bachelor of Fine Arts degree in Music Performance with bagpipes as the principal instrument.

Students have private studio instruction in bagpipes, professional training in bagpipe reed making, and learn maintenance and the history of the instrument. They must also participate in the choral program, complete instruction in music theory, solfège (applying the sol-fa syllables to a musical scale or melody), eurhythmics, music history, piano, and performing ensembles and a wide range of courses available as general studies electives.

Neuroscience   Given the wealth of new advanced imaging devices, the brain, with its infinite mystery, is an exciting focus of science today. That's why many universities, including Johns Hopkins University in Baltimore, added a new major, neuroscience, which links the many disciplines that investigate the nervous system. "People studying the brain realized that a lot of separate disciplines were interested in the brain, and they weren't talking to each other," said Gregory Ball, an academic advisor and psychology professor. "Some people were studying brain and behavior; some were studying neuroanatomy; some people were studying neurophysiology; some people were studying brain development."

The new program at Hopkins is divided into three parts: cognitive neuroscience, systems neuroscience, and cellular and molecular neuroscience. The first studies how the brain accomplishes cognitive function, such as language, memory, and perception. The second refers to how nerve cells are arranged in circuits or systems that control specific functions. The third studies how nerve cells work and communicate with one another.

"Part of the idea was to make a connection between the nuts and bolts of biology and some of the most exciting questions that life scientists are grappling with today," Ball said.

Electronic Media, Arts, and Communication

The first program of its kind anywhere in the country, Rensselaer Polytechnic Institute in Troy, New York, is offering a state-of-the-art electronic media, arts, and communication major. A hybrid of electronic communication and electronic art, it will train students for jobs in a cross-section of "virtual" industries, including game design, videography, multimedia production, virtual reality design, electronic arts and performance, infotainment, World Wide Web authoring, and animation.

This new type of interdisciplinary program aims to produce entrepreneurs who will use technology in innovative ways in industry and the arts. At Rensselaer, the goal is to train students for leadership in a rapidly transforming information society.

Technical Music

It's not enough that you know your scales and play an instrument well. As with so much of the techno-advanced society, music has been transformed. A place where you can go to learn more about it, even become an expert, is MiraCosta College in Oceanside, California. In the technical music program students compose, perform, and record in styles including classical, jazz, pop, and rock. In addition, they get hands-on experience using MIDI (musical instrument digital interface), which, when attached to a computer and a keyboard, allows them to compose, write, manipulate, and record music. They also work in the college's two recording studios, stocked with industry-standard equipment and open seven days a week.

Students annually produce a CD featuring local bands and hold concerts usually featuring one or more of these bands for which they do everything, including lighting, sound, promotion, and crowd management. After graduation students have become recording engineers and audio engineers. Others work in music retail, sound reinforcement in theaters, and live sound in churches. The major is directed by twin brothers, Dave and Don Megill, who also are music instructors.

Asian Studies
As the Internet and other forces shrink the globe economically and culturally, more information on Asia is available to interested students. At Bowdoin College in Brunswick, Maine, and other schools, interest in Asian studies has grown. At Bowdoin studies focus on the cultural traditions of either East Asia (China and Japan) or South Asia (India and Sri Lanka). Students in this major must study both cultural areas, acquire a working proficiency in one of the languages of South or East Asia, and become knowledgeable in one of the areas of study of the region: history, religion, literature, or anthropology. Students are encouraged to visit and study the area of their specialization. At Bowdoin all freshmen attend a first-year seminar program to familiarize them with the intellectual life of going to college. Students in the Asian Studies program may choose the following seminars for this year:

Religions of India in Contemporary Literature

Women in Japanese Culture

Women's Lives in South Asia

The First Emperor of China

The Cultural Revolution

Ethnic Studies
Social change has given birth to new majors on campus, highlighting different ethnic groups. Starting in the 1960s social and political unrest spawned Black and Chicano studies on campuses while Asian-American studies lagged. In the last few years interest has grown in the subject, particularly because of the contested California law on affirmative action. According to *The Chronicle of Higher Education* (May 31, 1996), Asian-American studies differ depending on which coast your college is located: on the West Coast, the courses focus on the gold rush or such contemporary topics as Asian-Black relations since the 1992 Los Angeles riots. On the East Coast, the publication states, the focus is international.

Look for More
You can see from reading about these new and unusual majors that a wide array of choices awaits students of every interest. Investigate on your own. Whether it's gerontology, the specialty of working with the aged, or musicology, colleges are dynamic places that incorporate change to serve the needs of students and society.

Design Your Own Major

At Sarah Lawrence College

There are no declared majors at Sarah Lawrence College, a liberal arts college for men and women in Bronxville, N.Y. Instead, with the help of an advisor (called a don), students design their own curricula.

Each student's program consists of three seminar courses of no more than 15 students, allowing for intensive study in each field. Students attend individual student-faculty meetings every other week. For each seminar, students complete a conference project—an independent study that results in a substantial research paper or project—in addition to their class work. Every course requires that students spend at least 15 hours weekly in study, for which they earn 10 semester hours of credit a year. Most courses are full-year courses.

Besides no majors, Sarah Lawrence has no finals or grades, unless these are needed for transfer or prior to graduate school or professional studies. Instead of grades, growth and achievement of the student are evaluated in reports written by faculty and sent to the students and their advisors twice a year. In these statements, faculty members report their judgment of the student's academic achievement, attitude toward work, study habits, ability to learn and form judgments and to use what is learned, ability to work independently—all the factors that show a student's intellectual progress.

Instead of finals, students submit a worksheet, a written bibliographic record of all work done during the semester, for each course. Students look over the worksheets and evaluate the entire year's work for themselves.

Meira Kensky got interested in Sarah Lawrence while watching television. She was captivated by the character Simone on the TV show, "Head of the Class." In the program, Simone went to Sarah Lawrence and was editor of a literary magazine, a poetry person, Kensky remembers. "I had no idea Sarah Lawrence didn't have majors until I visited," she said. Now a sophomore at Sarah Lawrence, where she is editor of the forum-based publication *Dialogue* and treasurer of the student senate, she is pleased with the freedom that the non-major program has provided. In her second semester there she wrote a 30-page paper on the freedom of religion clauses in the First Amendment, which involved designing the project and reading 40 to 50 Supreme Court opinions plus other articles.

"Here, everyone is writing papers all the time but feels free to take a studio art class or read Nabokov. We're involved in scholarship, not pre-track. If you want to know your grade point average, you can calculate it yourself or ask for it, but people aren't constantly freaking about grade point," she said.

This fall she'll be attending Wadham College, Oxford, and is uncertain whether she'll study Shakespeare, read Milton, or take a theology tutorial. Although she started out interested mainly in theater, her concentration now has shifted to the humanities.

At The Evergreen State College

Coordinated studies, in which students and faculty from different disciplines join to answer a question or solve a problem, are the beginning of academic life at The Evergreen State College in Olympia, Washington. In freshman and sophomore years students may choose among seven core programs.

For 1996–97 the programs at Evergreen were Asian Performing Arts and Culture, The Awakening Mind-Spirit, Ecological Systems of Puget Sound, Environmental Change and Health: Global Context, Regional Conditions, Great Works and What They're Made Of, Masculine and Feminine, and Search for Meaning. The purpose of the core approach is for students to learn the skills they will need for more advanced study, mainly writing, reading carefully, analyzing arguments, skillfully reasoning quantitatively or mathematically, working cooperatively with others, and using resources. The core program also allows students to connect studies with their own intellectual and personal concerns.

After completing the core program, students choose among specialty areas, which are topical groupings of academic offerings planned by a group of faculty with similar interests. Under Knowledge and the Human Condition, for instance, are listed

Science, Art and Ideology in Social Context

Feminist Studies/Cultural Studies

The Fool's Journey: Exploring and Designing Paths to Appropriate Work and Leadership

Public Education

Religion and Social Change

Six Months with Shakespeare: Interdisciplinary Studies of His Works and World

Literary Journalism

Meditations on Nature, Human and Otherwise

Student Originated Studies in Humanities and Social Sciences

Hemingway

Prose Workshop

The Vanishing Father

The Lottery: Ticket to Trouble?

Oral History: Theory and Practice

Poetry

Schopenhauer

Writers' Workshop

Restorying the American West

Victorian Studies: British Culture and Society 1837–1901

Turn of the Century: Government and Society, 1900 and 2000

Writing Process/Writing Product

Hype and Hucksters: Media Campaigns as Popular Culture

Bones and Stones, the Roots of Society: Achievements of Our Prehistoric Ancestors

The English Romantics: Poetry and Fiction, Wordsworth to Scott

Tempting the Muse: The Language of Poetry "Tenter las muse: le langage de las poesie"

Life as Art: Art as Life: Advanced Studies in Surrealism

Orientalism and Afrocentricity: En-Countering the Master Narrative

Senior Seminar

A description of the course "A Fool's Journey: Exploring and Designing Paths to Appropriate Work and Leadership" reads:

There is work of your own to do
You will never reach the end of your becoming
The madness of creation
The joy of existence.
                                        —Normandi Ellis

The description continues:

> Students who are serious about seeking ways
> to work honestly and reflectively in the world
> are welcome to join. We will work together to
> see what other seekers have to offer to an
> understanding of designing a life's work in
> social and cultural context. We will do this
> work in a community of tolerance and support
> for each other. This program will focus on
> cross-cultural work in the world; during the
> first quarter of our work we will read together,
> talk and write. We will read Thich Nat Hanh,
> J. G. Bennett, The Dalai Lama and Thomas
> Merton, and from books such as the Aramaic
> New Testament in translation and the *Cries of
> the Spirit* by Marilyn Sewell. We will examine
> perspectives from texts such as *The Most
> Beautiful House in the World*, *The Unknown
> Craftsman* and *Number Our Days*. During the
> second quarter, students and faculty will
> spend one month in independent work of their
> choosing, based upon the direction they
> develop from reading, writing, and meditation
> in the fall. The last six weeks of the quarter
> will focus on bringing the results of personal
> journeys back to community as action and
> commitment.

The other specialty areas at Evergreen are environmental studies, expressive arts, language and culture, management studies, Native American studies, political economy and social change, science and human values, and science, technology, and health.

Students plan an academic pathway with an advisor and may work for a number of quarters within one specialty area or may move from area to area to broaden their education.

The college reminds students that "Besides thinking about what you want to know, you must also think about what it takes to learn what you want to know." The example cited is a student interested in migratory bird habitats. Such a student needs to know about ornithology and ecology, environmental policy and the political process, "something about the history of ecological policy and the development of the West, something about the ways people have talked and felt about land use and conservation, something about the fundamental ways humans perceive the space around them."

At Marlboro College

A small and innovative liberal arts college in Vermont, Marlboro offers each student a highly individualized program of study. Students design their own majors, and most of them are multidisciplinary. Recent students have combined biology and theater, international studies and dance, creative writing and sociology.

One of the newer colleges in the United States, Marlboro College was founded in 1946 by a handful of veterans who transformed two Vermont Hill farms into classrooms, dorms, and a dining hall. The original student body of 50 has grown to include 280 students who come to Vermont for individualized education.

The academic program is based on the Plan of Concentration, a two-year program in which students explore a field of interest and conclude with a major independent project that aims to solve a problem or answer a question of vital interest to the student. Students work with faculty in one-on-one individualized tutorials designed to instruct them in an area not normally covered in the regular course schedule. Before graduation students must defend their plans in a two- or three-hour oral exam before Marlboro faculty members and an outside examiner from another institution who is expert in the subject area of the plan.

"I came to Marlboro not knowing what my major would be. After I took the course in desert biology and went on the desert field trip, I knew what I wanted to do. The work I did on my Plan got me started doing research long before I entered graduate school," is a testimonial provided by Peter Niewiarowski, class of 1984, who subsequently earned his doctorate in evolutionary biology at the University of Pennsylvania.

Stop, Look, and Consider Your Many Choices

If you don't think you will fit into a traditional curriculum, and no major feels "right," a design-your-own major may be the best choice. Ask at each school whether such an option is available.

Choose a Major, Then Concentrate on Skills

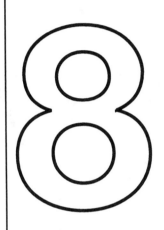

Choosing a major is merely choosing a label to wear on campus. With less matching today between majors and careers, college career counselors are advising students to concentrate on skill development. "The world appreciates smart people, but they need to develop transferable skills," said a career counselor. "The skills are theirs wherever they go," she added.

Skill development should run parallel to a thorough understanding of your major. Many of the skills will be yours merely by rubbing shoulders on campus with professors and the other students and completing course work. Others, such as the feared presentation skills, will require a concerted effort on your part to develop before you finish school.

Today, skills have become the gold standard for success in whatever you choose to do after graduation. The 38-year-old returning student gets A's instead of the C's she earned at age twenty because life has taught her important skills.

Review the following skills considered important for a successful future. Determine which ones you already have and which ones you need to develop. Your years on campus will provide many opportunities to add these skills to your proverbial bag of tricks.

Critical Thinking Skills

Critical thinking uses information, reason, and experience to move from assumptions to applications to consequences. College students develop critical thinking because of the amount of research required of them. Once you investigate any subject you find it is much more complicated than it appeared at first.

Building critical thinking skills means shedding preconceived notions. Shedding these notions opens the opportunity to look at a subject from a fresh perspective.

An important part of building critical thinking skills is gathering information and judging which sources are valid. In the college experience students read writings of many authors and hear lectures offering different viewpoints. In the dorms and in classrooms you will hear opinions much different from your own. In writing research papers you must decide which position to take, find supporting arguments, and provide documentation. Critical thinking continues for the rest of your life. Developing this skill in college is a major task.

Presesentation Skills

"I get too nervous to get up in front of a group of people and talk."

As painful as the news might be, you are going to have to learn to speak in front of a group. You may have already done this in high school and in a few classes in college. Few people automatically feel comfortable speaking in front of a group. David Letterman said in an interview that his ego rises and falls on each night's performance. The best ideas in the world get lost if individuals can't present their ideas in front of other people. Some students, however, would rather have their hair pulled out than say a word in class.

Richard, a stutterer in high school, readily volunteers his ideas in classroom discussions today. He achieved this, he says, by forcing himself to make speeches and speaking up whenever he saw an opportunity. He made up his mind to attack this problem and now presents verbally better than most college seniors.

Getting your ideas across in classroom discussions, in conferences with instructors, and in team projects establishes their validity. You give other people an opportunity to react to what you've said.

Understanding the nuances of words and expressions, body language, the appropriateness of behaviors—these are skills that students learn more fully in college, mainly by interacting with many different people. To develop excellent presentation skills, you must:

1. Develop something interesting to say: something original, thought-provoking, and entertaining

2. Understand the needs of your audience, whether it's one person or many

3. Practice whenever you get a chance

Listening Skills

Pay attention. Much of learning goes on through listening. In large lecture halls, in study groups, in one-on-one conversations, the ability to listen intently to the information being given is important for success both in college and later in the much longer career years. When someone is talking, the rest may be thinking about what they are going to say next instead of really capturing what the speaker is saying. A good way to enhance your listening skills is to devote one day to really listening to whatever people are saying. People appreciate being heard.

The Written Word

Writing is one of the most tangible forms of expression. Many opportunities present themselves in college for writing and improving your writing, especially at the college's writing center and in individual conferences with instructors in the English department. You will learn more fully how to identify the needs of your audience, focus, have something important to say, and present your ideas in a logical progression.

Published authors do many drafts and revisions and much soul-searching to get the right words on paper. Authors read to see how other writers present ideas. If you don't master writing, it will cripple your career. The good news is that the more you write, the better you will get. Unfortunately, the people most needing to develop this skill are afraid to write and be critiqued. Practice makes perfect, or at least, better. In questionnaires where employees are asked what they dislike about work, "writing" is one of tasks they hate the most.

Writing forces you to concentrate, revise, hammer out what you wish to say to your audience. The process takes time. And it's lonely. To improve your writing ability, take as many writing courses as you can. Here are some quick tips:

1. Use concrete nouns for subjects of sentences instead of vague and often pretentious words. Consider *school* instead of *institution*; *club* instead of *organization*.

2. Put the focal point at the beginning of the sentence, avoiding "There is," "There are," or "It is."

3. Use specifics instead of generalizations. Don't skimp on information.

4. Build a vocabulary of strong verbs instead of relying on forms of *to be: is, am, are*.

5. Draft, draft, draft.

You cannot become a good writer by yourself. The mind requires the nourishment of new ideas and reading in order to produce good writing. Even half an hour a day devoted to reading for your own growth as a writer is well worth the effort. If you need inspiration, read *Bird by Bird: Some Instructions on Writing and Life* by Anne Lamott.

Don't Stumble Over Spelling

The ability to spell words correctly has nothing to do with intelligence or the ability to solve problems. With the introduction of spelling checkers in computer programs, much of the anxiety has been eliminated. Another way around the problem is to have a reader, someone who will read your work to check for spelling and grammatical errors. The second pair of eyes also will catch any crazy ideas you may have written.

Phone Skills

In an effort to save money, many companies today conduct the first interview with a prospective employee over the phone. Frequently people get eliminated at this early stage in the process because they have not developed good phone skills.

Enthusiasm is an important phone skill. Many opportunities will be lost if you sound uninterested when a potential employer calls. Most recent graduates are very interested, but astonished that their resumes actually prompted a phone call. The shock makes it hard to recover. Or the person is nervous. Before the call comes, practice answering with a positive voice and sounding receptive to the company. If you don't think you are at your best form when the call comes, offer to call the interviewer back in an hour. Say "This is not a good time to talk. May I return your call in an hour?" Interviewers will not be offended, as long as you do call back.

Another part of phone skill is clarity. When leaving a message, don't zoom over the return phone number. Polished professionals repeat the number they are leaving twice. This can save everyone a great deal of time and is part of phone skill.

In building this skill, have friends critique how you sound over the phone. One job applicant was discarded from the pile of resumes on the basis of his haughty-sounding tone on his answering machine. The goal is to sound friendly and positive. Also, if you are sending out resumes or expecting other important calls, make sure the message on your answering machine is appropriate. Don't let a humorous message intended for your friends make a poor first impression on an important caller.

Background noise can also give the wrong impression. When you answer the phone be sure to turn off the radio and television. The Smashing Pumpkins in the background may be distracting to the caller. How many times have you called and heard a dog barking in the background? Then the person you are calling interrupts the conversation repeatedly to tell the dog to be quiet. Obviously, this does not project a professional, in-charge image. You can't even manage a dog, the caller thinks, although perhaps only subconsciously. Excuse yourself briefly and remove the dog from the room.

Having paper and pencil by the phone is part of phone skill. Waiting while you run upstairs to get writing supplies wastes the caller's time. Call waiting also wastes the time of the person on the phone with you. Let the call wait, not the person with whom you are talking.

Professionals return most phone messages the day they are received. They also respond promptly to invitations. Not responding to calls or invitations is considered the work of an amateur in the world of professionals.

E-mail Skills   People who normally write excellent letters with perfect spelling take all sorts of liberty with e-mail. This does not promote a good impression. Merely because e-mail is new and the speed is like lightening does not mean that messages should be written without care. Be sure to read your e-mail messages carefully before they go out. Skill in e-mailing is part of the parcel of a complete professional. Warning: On e-mail, don't accidentally press the button that says "Reply to all respondents." Many people have stories about how a highly personal memo was sent electronically to a group of people who did not need to be provided with this information.

Interpersonal Skills   No matter how brilliant people are, they will be lost without interpersonal skills, the ability to get along with other people. In his best-selling book *Emotional Intelligence*, Daniel Goleman says that achievers reach success by building a rapport with a network of key people who can be relied on when expert help is needed. In a crunch, these people have contacts. He writes:

> But after detailed interviews, the critical differences emerged in the internal and interpersonal strategies "stars" used to get their work done. One of the most important turned out to be a rapport with a network of key people. Things go more smoothly for the standouts because they put time into cultivating good relationships with people whose services might be needed in a crunch as part of an instant ad hoc team to solve a problem or handle a crisis.

Shedding any shyness or self-consciousness left over from adolescence is part of the college experience. Ways to do this? Start talking to other people in class and begin to form study groups. Working together with other people on projects is the foundation of being a good team member later. Studying together makes understanding the material infinitely easier. Human beings need each other. College is a natural time to start developing interpersonal skills.

Interpersonal skills, then, are a major learning task in college. Colleges are aware of the importance of these skills. Coincidentally, these skills serve the colleges' purpose of retention, keeping students enrolled. One of the prime reasons students stay at the college they selected is a sense of belonging. If they feel comfortable and can afford the tuition, they will stay. Whether this sense of belonging comes from joining the rock climbing club, a sorority, or great freshman roommates, students decide to return, saving the college a great deal of effort and recruitment funds.

You can test your own interpersonal skills by asking yourself the following questions:

1. Have you met any interesting new people in the past three months?

2. Have you made an effort to get to know them better?

3. Do you write letters or e-mail to people on a regular basis?

4. Do you count on other people for new ideas?

5. Can you think of ways to make your life more interesting? Do these include other people?

Networking Skills

The students most resistant to developing networking skills are those who feel they have to accomplish everything on their own. Somehow, they feel it is poor form to ask for help.

People need networks to live. They need networks to find lifetime partners, find jobs, keep jobs, keep functioning, survive. Making friends makes the business of living easier. The whole is greater than the sum of its parts. People working together are more creative, get a lot more done, and according to studies, live longer, than people who are the archetypical loners. In a system of social beings, loners lose.

Networking means connecting to many different individuals. One person's network may include a dog groomer, an IRS agent, a police officer, an airline reservationist, and a retired dentist. Each has special skills and important gifts to share. Staying in touch with interesting people you meet, either with a postcard, an e-mail, a phone call, or over coffee is the basis for networking.

Some people are natural networkers, weaving people

into all aspects of their lives and welcoming the diversity. But even if it doesn't come naturally, the skill of networking can be developed.

Imagine that you were asked to produce a cable television program on the subject of America's work habits. You will need people from all ages and walks of life to talk about what they do at work. Relying on the people you already know, how many occupations could they provide you with, using their friends and families?

Organizational Skills

How would you label yourself today? Very organized? Disorganized? The American culture values organized people and gives them higher salaries. Rewards go to individuals who come early to meetings, hand projects in on time, have backup plans in case the first one falls in the ditch. These organized people are valued as a rare commodity. Why? If you asked ten people to give a pint of blood to your friend, wouldn't you value the ones who showed up on time, gave blood, and saved your friend's life? Having organizational skills means being the one people can count on to get things done. You anticipate the problems, you have a goal, you meet the deadline. How do you become organized? Not overnight. Like other new skills, it takes time. One way to become organized is to evaluate your reaction mode. In plain English, do you react to and act on everything? If you do, you are not organized. A million demands hit us every day. Prioritizing them is the basis of organizational skill. Organization simply means knowing what is important to you and sticking to it.

Begin with a simple test. Are you always on time, always late, or always early? Why? If you can answer that question, you are on your way to discovering your organizational strengths and weaknesses.

Let's say good grades are your priority this semester but you are also a social being with lots of temptations to party. You have to make up your mind: grades or fun? Usually, the reality is somewhere in the middle. Compromise. Disorganized people, however, are in an all-or-nothing mode. They become disorganized because they throw out the goal for a new pursuit. Sticking with goals is not easy. When temptations come, the organized person accepts them partially without going overboard.

Staying on track in the face of interruptions is a major part of organizational skills. Happily, organizational skills improve the longer you are in college. They must or you would flunk out. You learn how to boomerang back to your main task after several interruptions. You learn how to prioritize to tackle the most important tasks first. Some college graduates feel that the diploma is a sign of mastering organizational skills, or, they learned to jump nimbly through many hoops.

Know Your Rhythm

Knowing your own body rhythm is a part of getting organized. If there are times of the day or month when you are not at your peak, you know not to overload responsibilities at those times.

Notebooks and Calendars

Not too very long ago people could keep important dates and notes of things to do in their heads. Rarely is this the case today. Our environment is too crowded with stimuli for us to remember everything. Even 18-year-olds have to write down dates and reminders.

Particularly helpful are the pocket-size computer notebooks that keep phone numbers, addresses, important dates, and messages to yourself.

Most very organized people write the next day's plan the night before. Making a stress-avoidance plan at the first of the month helps ease some of the frustrations, parking tickets, and missed appointments so common in a fast-paced society.

Realism about Time

Unrealistic ideas about how much time it takes to complete a task are the cornerstone of disorganization. These ideas include misjudged travel time, weather conditions, and study requirements and usually err on the side of underestimation. Everything takes more time than most people estimate. What you think will take two hours takes four. Time is a precious commodity that is sorely underestimated and undervalued.

The Twin Thieves of Television and Netsurfing

Hours of valuable time can drift away in front of a television or surfing the Net. Rare is the person who spends less than five hours a week in front of one of these screens. They may be useful, entertaining, enlightening, even educational, but they do distract the person who's inclined to be disorganized.

Research Skills

You won't be able to graduate from college without research skills. Merely figuring out what classes to take demands research. During the first semester freshman year students learn to gather material from sources other than the classroom and write about it. Today, researching means having computer research skills as well as being able to interview people for information.

Reading a newspaper regularly will increase your research skills. Americans are notorious for not knowing geography and being unaware of foreign events. Most newspapers ignore this flaw and report events of the world every day. Particularly with globalization, knowing about the world and the activities of people outside your own sphere of influence increases your ability to conduct research. A broad range of knowledge help you determine what is important to investigate and what can be cast aside.

The world is too complex and sophisticated for you to know about everything. The newspaper is similar to a flashlight, illuminating things you should pay attention to, even for a few seconds. The mind keeps this information and brings it up when you need it to build information in research.

Libraries and information sources are changing so rapidly that it's important to keep up on the latest ways to gather research. Instead of being overwhelmed by how much is out there, remember that you only need to know what is relevant for your field. You don't need to know everything.

Gaining a Professional Vocabulary

Your major will provide you with the skill of a professional vocabulary. Every washing machine repair person in the United States uses the same terminology, which is a foreign language to everyone else. Every major has its own language. Biologists use words such as *photomorphogenesis, convergence, macromolecules,* and *clonal segments.* Chemists talk about *reactivity* and *kinetics.* English majors use *rhetoric, discourse,* and *genre.* Whichever major you choose, you will gain the skill of using a professional vocabulary. In job interviews, the interviewer will expect you to be familiar with the vocabulary of your specialty. No problem.

Concentration

Older people say the younger generation has lost its attention span. They blame it on MTV. They remember when reading and radio were the principal forms of entertainment and television did not consume many hours of the day. When the work was done, they talked to their neighbors on the porch, played cards, shot pool at the corner saloon, made pies, did homework. Homework assignments were simpler and easier to do because there weren't as many distractions. The old folks didn't have VCRs, microwave ovens, cellular phones, answering machines, or credit cards. If they are correct, the ability to concentrate on what you want to learn is more difficult to achieve than in the past.

In college you will develop the skill of concentration, the ability you need to gain new knowledge. Does retention require you to review the material once? Three times? Sixteen times? How much time does it take you to acquire new knowledge? What is the optimal setting for you to acquire this knowledge? Do you need low background music to keep you focused? Or do you need complete quiet? Do you need to study in the library to stay away from your friends?

Knowing how to concentrate is extremely helpful in your life after college. A swirl of information will hit you most days in the work world and you need to be able to concentrate on what is important to you.

Coachability

Coachability, the ability to be coached, is a new term in education and job environments. If you are able to be coached into higher performance, you possess coachability. Some people refuse to listen to those higher than them in authority. No matter what the directions are, they decide to do it their own way. Organizations run best with people who are willing to be coached.

A first good place to learn and build coachability skills is in college, although some people learn the skill in high school. The skill is not only doing what you have been asked to do, but also figuring out what the coach wants done without being told. The second is much more difficult. The people who get As in the classroom often have an innate sense of what is important to study, what the professor cares about and what is irrelevant in the professor's mind. These people are also the good test takers because they know what is important to study without having to review everything.

People who have good coachability skills follow directions easily and do not complain about workload. They seem to be motivated to get the job done with a minimum of confusion. They are pleasant to be around because they are positive and goal oriented. They also are flexible. In a fast-changing world people have to adjust frequently to change. The coach (professor, boss) gives one set of directions one week, and because of circumstances, changes them the next week. The coachable person knows that game plans change.

People with coachability skills do well in college because they accept the format of college and comply with the rules. This includes:

1. Attending class regularly
2. Buying the textbooks required
3. Handing in assignments on time
4. Keeping track of what is due and when
5. Talking with the instructor when assignments or classes are not clear
6. Seeing advisors about graduating on time
7. Thinking of ways to fit in rather than causing academic problems for themselves
8. Hearing what the rules are and following them
9. Quickly becoming familiar with the terrain and adapting
10. Being a member of a team and not trying to usurp the coach's rules

Creativity

College takes people out of what they have known into an exploration of the unknown. Individual families, communities, and high schools all support a common culture. Once you leave that arena and go off to college, even if it is a few blocks away, the expectations and possibilities change.

The knowledge not only of what is, but of what can be, is developed through a college education. The skill of creating something new, whether it's in a test tube, on the printed page in a poem, or in a marketing program for a widget is a byproduct of higher education. Walking across campus gives students the time to be away from the "real world." This escape provides time for original thoughts, new ways of doing old things, or thinking of new ideas to advance civilization.

"What if . . ." becomes the mantra taken after graduation to offices, homes, Web pages, and board rooms. To leave college without a heightened sense of the freedom to be creative means you haven't learned an important skill there.

Technological Skills

Almost every freshman orientation includes exposure to the computer facilities on campus. But many of these facilities are underutilized by students who are computer phobic. It takes tremendous discipline to spend time each week in the computer facility learning about new programs. Some students give up too easily. Computer mastery takes many hours and can be discouraging unless you are willing to accept the fact that this new technology takes time.

You need to know where to find information available through the Internet, how to evaluate and document it. The main task is to overcome computer phobia and realize that the learning curve on any program is very short—in two weeks you could learn all you need to know for any particular program. Second, realize that you don't need to know everything that's out there. The 17-year-old computer wiz at the local high school will do that (and little else). You only need to know the programs essential for your coursework and field of study.

The Paperless Society

Preparing for a paperless society is the goal today, according to Keith Dorwick, an educational technologist, one of those people who prepare educational institutions for the technological future.

"The minimum skill needed is the effective and thorough use of e-mail, with care not to send a message to everyone on your listserve, which can be embarrassing," he said. "Students should know how to attach files and decode them. They should know one computer language, even if it's only HTML (hypertext markup language), and the relationship between clients and servers. It's important to know one collaborative program," he said, "so that you can hook up several computers to share a project." Dorwick's dream of the future is all students having laptop computers included in the cost of tuition. Then everyone will have access to the same level of computer literacy.

Planning Skills

College forces you to plan. The syllabus gives you a whole semester or quarter to look at the first day of class or the first day it's posted on the school's Web page. After recovering from the shock of how many books, reports, or projects you'll have to read or do, you will make a plan, or should make a plan. When you see the date that midterms occur, you will realize not to plan an overnight camping trip or a bicycle weekend at the same time.

To fail to plan is to plan to fail. A familiar axiom in corporate offices and political campaigns, the need to plan becomes immediately obvious to college students. For some in technical specialties, such as engineering and computer science, there is little space for electives outside of the specialty. Unfortunately, some students plan their courses up to graduation and have no clue of how this plan will fit in with their future lives. A leftover impression from early days is that a college degree will somehow confer upon an individual a passport for life and that graduation itself is the goal.

College must incorporate planning skills. The people who do not learn these skills are easy to spot: they drop out. It's safe to say that if you have gotten to college, decided on a major, pursued it, and graduated, you have achieved some expertise at planning.

Accountability

Many upper-level courses in college today involve team projects. The team is judged as a whole and the team members each receive the same grade. It quickly becomes apparent which team members are not willing to pull their load. Usually the other team members put up with this and fill in the gap. The instructor leaves the discipline of the team to team members. Figuring out how to motivate the noncontributing member is part of the work of being on a team.

The benefit of these exercises is to show students how things occur in the "real" world. Students on the team who shun accountability incur hostility and animosity from other team members. Teams are currently in vogue in the workplace, and college is an excellent time to get experience in the ways teams work.

Perception

Observing people, events, speeches, groups, and interactions form an important part of the college experience. Kiosks and bulletin boards inform students daily of opportunities to hear guest speakers, attend forums and concerts, debates, athletic events, and symposiums. Through this vast exposure on campus you will have the opportunity to weigh different viewpoints, explore the differences, and increase your ability to perceive. Besides the vast public exposure, students hear the voices of professors offering views they may have never previously considered.

Tolerance

A diverse workforce is essential for America to remain competitive in the world. Students who have been raised in urban or suburban ghettos where everyone is the same racially, economically, and religiously will be at a disadvantage in preparing for the future. Bringing people of different backgrounds together to be productive is a valuable skill. Most colleges try to obtain a diverse population in their application process, but frequently, upon graduation, students are shocked culturally with the attitudes and customs of the workforce they are asked to manage or collaborate with.

Seeking out people who are different from you on campus will round out your education. Foreign students have much to add to your knowledge of the world. A fellow student might tell you, for instance, that in his country, a man is allowed to have two wives and families if he can support both financially. Or that in her country there is no set schedule for mail to arrive, it might come every four days and then not again for a few weeks. American students benefit from knowing that countries vary enormously in their ways of interacting and living.

Coping Skills

With all the ups and downs of life on campus, coping skills put you in a prepared position no matter what happens. The computer loses the grades, the counselor forgot to tell you about a course you need for graduation, the instructor didn't mention that he wanted MLA documentation on the research paper and you have to completely redo the citations. These events are good because they teach you how to cope. The skills you learn—politeness, patience, investigation of other ways to accomplish your task—will enrich your life on the outside. Knowing how to cope, no matter what happens, is a fundamental skill to learn on campus. Most people won't graduate without it.

Initiative and Leadership

The tendency to hesitate too long and think of reasons you shouldn't move ahead needs to be overcome. Initiative and leadership skills mean acknowledging that mistakes will be made but not having regrets for chances missed. Initiative means going for it, catching the train, jumping on the bandwagon, following the calliope. In the words of Nike, it means "Just Do It."

Perseverance

"There are doers and there are stewers" is a saying Robert Dole, presidential contender, learned from his father in Kansas. The lesson he learned at home helped him through massive injuries suffered in the Second World War that eliminated hope he had of being a surgeon and started him on the path to becoming a senator.

Most students today will not be facing the prospect of war on foreign soil, but working toward a degree does prove whether you have the stamina to finish a job started. Employers want to know that you can jump through the hoops that college demands. In some classes the instructor won't speak English clearly, in others you won't have a clue of what is being written on the board or shown on the overhead. You will face final exams that cover too much material for anyone's brain capacity. You will have poor teachers who would rather not spend time in the classroom and don't have office hours.

Surely these situations are not as bad as Dole's having his body severely injured in Italy and three years of painful rehabilitation to recover. But sometimes, college will feel awful. That's where the skill of perseverance will come in.

How will you know if you have developed this skill in college? You will receive a piece of paper called a diploma that attests to your skill of perseverance. With this piece of paper you will become a college graduate. This tells people that you have achieved a level of perseverance, no matter how long it has taken. For this, you deserve congratulations.

Jobs for the 21st Century

Life without change would be exceedingly boring. Careers have been anything but boring in the last ten years with downsizing and delayering. The days of gold watches for fifty years of service are gone and the exciting challenge of many careers in a lifetime is here.

Choosing a major in this state of transition is tricky, but as stated in earlier chapters, it's the skills you learn through the major that are important, not the major itself. The major has to be an area that interests you enough to study for four or more years, and one that has meaning in your life.

That said, what are the experts saying about jobs in the future? To blindly choose a major with no thought to its future application is foolhardy. So, what are the experts saying? With the caveat that experts have been wrong in the past, the experts are saying that three main factors will impact the job market: an aging population

165

and health consciousness, trade across the globe, and advancing technology. Not surprisingly these factors have a profound effect on the job market.

Who Knows Better than Your Uncle Sam?

The main source of information on the future of the job market is the U.S. Department of Labor, Bureau of Labor Statistics (BLS) and its *Occupational Outlook Handbook*, available in most libraries. This government bureau bases its projections on U.S. Census Bureau information. In addition, information is gathered from trade associations, professional societies, unions, industrial organizations, and government agencies. The government cannot guarantee, however, that any information it receives from these sources is 100 percent accurate.

Twenty years ago the BLS accurately projected engineering as the hot major. Students graduating with degrees in engineering were getting four and five job offers. Back then, computer programmers and systems analysts had little sparkle; they were classified with the numbers for office jobs, such as stenographers and stock clerks.

The BLS did predict that by the mid-1980s expertise in computer technology would be a valuable commodity in the marketplace. The following is a synopsis of what the book says about the trends and jobs that hold the most promise for today's college students.

From now until the year 2005, the fastest growing positions for graduates with a bachelor's degree will be:

> Systems analysts
>
> Computer engineers
>
> Occupational therapists
>
> Physical therapists
>
> Special education teachers
>
> Teachers, secondary and elementary school levels
>
> Social workers

As you can see from this list, the hot new area will be services, not goods. Businesses, the aging, people in schools and hospitals, and those recuperating at home will all need service in unprecedented numbers. The American economy is shifting from a manufacturing focus to a service-providing focus.

According to the U.S. Bureau of Labor Statistics, the following is the ranking of fastest growing occupations requiring education beyond high school:

Occupation	Percent Change 1994–2005
Systems engineer	92
Computer engineer	90
Physical therapist	80
Residential counselor	72
Occupational therapist	72
Special education teacher	53
Operations research analyst	50
Speech-language pathologist	46
Employment interviewer	36
Management analyst	35

The fastest growing areas reflect the new employment needs in computer technology and health services. Some compare the present era to the Industrial Revolution in terms of gigantic change. This requires students to adapt also. If getting a job is the reason you are going to college, then the list provides the latest information available on job opportunities.

Taking care of patients in their homes is a booming industry as hospitals and insurance companies mandate shorter stays for operations, childbirth, and heart attack recovery. As companies move into home health care, many people—degreed and nondegreed—will be involved. This growing industry will need managers with business degrees as well as aides with high school educations.

Students who elect to major in any of the computer-related disciplines will have many opportunities to advance their skills in the exploding computer industry. However, careers in computer-related fields also involve a great deal of turbulence with companies going out of business and new ones being created.

Women will continue to gain in numbers in the workforce, comprising 48 percent of the labor force by the year 2005.

Look in Your Own Backyard

While federal labor statistics give specific industry growth, part of the data may not apply to your particular region or the region in which you hope to work and live someday. To find information specifically by state, contact the State

Occupational Information Coordinating Committee (SOICC), very often located in the state capital.

Another resource suggested by the Department of Labor is the state employment security agency, which can provide information about local labor markets, such as current and projected employment by occupation and industry, characteristics of the workforce, and changes in state and local area economic activity. These state employment security agencies have different names. For example, in Idaho, it's the Idaho Department of Employment, in Colorado it's called the Colorado Department of Labor. Check the front of your phone book for your individual state's listing.

A third resource at the state level, recommended by the Department of Labor, is career information delivery systems (CIDS) available in high schools, colleges, and libraries. Job seekers can access information via computers, printed material, microfiche, and toll-free hotlines.

The Big Problem with Trends

While sitting in a library in snowy Vermont, you may be reading about job trends for the future in California. The problem with this is the unforeseen events that can happen, such as the end of the Cold War, which threw many people in California out of jobs as the defense industry shrank. The best you can do is take an educated guess, based on lots of research. Government documents are not exciting reading material, but soon you adapt to the style and very quickly you will start finding useful information.

The Department of Labor Projections

The Department of Labor describes the following jobs as having at least average growth in the future. Some are very competitive. You may not have considered some of these listed.

Accountants

As long as there are taxes, profits, and losses, there will be a need for accountants. But the profession is changing. Rules are becoming more complex, and although you can practice without a license, increasingly, employers are requiring a master's degree. States are in the process of adapting a 150-hour degree requirement before taking the Certified Public Accounting exam, making this professional level harder to attain.

Budget Analysts   As complicated as this name may sound, it merely means planning a budget, just as you and your parents have for your college expenses. As a professional, you would plan a budget for private industry, a nonprofit organization, or in the public sector. If you like working alone, this is the perfect job because most of the time is spent reviewing numbers. The increase in demand for budget analysts will be offset by increasing competition for the jobs.

Employment Interviewers   The outlook for these job brokers is bright. Acting as the connection between people looking for a job and organizations offering jobs, employment interviewers will find many opportunities for work as employment is expected to grow much faster than the average of all occupations through the year 2005.

Financial Managers   Everyone is a financial manager, but for those who do it for a living, the prospects are good. But the competition will be tough. Only those with highly honed skills need apply. This means those most skilled, adaptable, and knowledgeable will get the jobs. Financial managers prepare the reports required by firms to conduct their operations and to satisfy tax and regulatory requirements. These people also oversee the flow of cash and financial instruments, monitor the extension of credit, assess the risk of transactions, raise capital, analyze investments, keep an eye on the future financial status of the firm, and communicate with stockholders.

Students who graduate with degrees in accounting or finance are hired to work in the offices of financial management, but an MBA is required to advance.

Health Services Managers   Managing services for people in nursing homes and medical offices is the entry level position for this career, but an advanced degree is required to go any further. As health services continue to expand and diversify, the field of health services is expected to grow faster than the average for all occupations through the year 2005.

Hotel Managers   The future looks good for people who major in hotel management. This is one area where experience working for hotels and restaurants during high school and college is a plus in the preprofessional category. More than 160 colleges and universities offer bachelor and graduate degrees in the field.

Loan Officers

As the economy and population grow, the task of preparing, analyzing, and verifying loan applications will increase, making this a growing profession. Most of these positions require a degree in finance, economics, or a related field.

Management Consultants

All the expertise a company needs may not be on its payroll. Individuals working for management consultant companies assess the needs of their customer companies and make recommendations for increased productivity, efficiency, or saleability of a product. Or, a large company may need help reorganizing its corporate structure after acquiring a new division. Half of the people working in management consulting are self-employed. The growth of this occupation is projected to be higher than the average as industries increasingly rely on outside expertise to improve the performance of their organizations. Advancing competition from foreign markets has required American business operations to streamline and cut costs. Hiring outside consultants has been one way to get temporary help without putting additional personnel on the payroll. Almost every field uses outside consultants.

Marketing, Advertising, and Public Relations Managers

Identifying or creating demand for goods or services is the main job of these professionals, who have a bright employment outlook through the year 2005, according to the Labor Department. As companies have eliminated these departments in the 90s downsizing, they will hire outside companies to make up these services without having to hire permanent staff. Many employers require a broad liberal arts background with the majors of sociology, psychology, literature, or philosophy acceptable. Employment of these professionals is expected to increase faster than the average for all occupations through the year 2005.

Human Resources Professionals

When you answer a job ad in the newspaper you first meet the people in human resources. These are described by the Department of Labor as ones who recruit and interview employees and advise the company on whether an individual should be hired. They must know the policies and regulations that are the guidelines in their company as well as the laws that govern hiring. They are supposed to be very personable, putting prospective employees at ease. They are the screeners, determining which applicants fit the company's needs.

They also are the trainers of employees, teaching them new skills and policies in a classroom or seminar setting. They are crucial to employees feeling as if they are part of an organized team. In this capacity, they must be expert communicators. They serve an important role in explaining the complexity of the work environment today as factors rapidly change and new knowledge is added.

Also included in this category are the compensation managers, those people who administer salaries in a fair and equitable manner. Through surveys they keep an eye on salaries at other similar companies. Similarly, another group, called employee benefit managers, handle the health insurance and benefit plans. These areas have become extremely complex as employer-provided benefits account for a growing proportion of overall compensation costs.

Managers of Employee Assistance Plans (EAPs) are responsible for all those areas that support the productivity of the employees, such as safety, health, first aid, security, publications, food service, recreation, car pooling, suggestion systems, child and elder care, and counseling services.

In any workplace there will be disputes over fairness. The specialists who work in this area are called industrial relations experts, whose job titles range from director of industrial relations to mediator. In the baseball strike, the harried, exhausted person trying to bring both sides to compromise was the mediator or arbitrator. Entry level in this field requires a college degree in human resources, personnel administration, labor or industrial relations, business, or liberal arts. The people in top management positions in this field have advanced degrees. The Department of Labor predicts faster than average growth for this category of jobs in the future.

Property and Real Estate Managers

The day-to-day management of apartment buildings, offices, and retail and industrial properties falls to the professional property managers. They are responsible for securing acceptable tenants, negotiating leases, establishing rental rates, collecting the rents, and paying the mortgages, taxes, insurance premiums, payroll, and maintenance bills on time. They prepare reports so that the owners of the property are informed of its financial status. If the property is a condominium the property manager must deal with the owners and the association of the owners.

College graduates are preferred for this category of jobs, with majors in business administration, real estate management, finance, public administration, or liberal arts. Jobs in this area are projected to increase as fast as the average in the next several years.

Restaurant and Food Service Managers

Behind the scenes of a restaurant or cafeteria is the multitalented food service manager. Just as other occupations have grown in complexity, the job of the food service manager has become very diverse, including labor relations, food supply, equipment maintenance, customer satisfaction, computer expertise, and financial accountability. As the Department of Labor notes, "Managers are among the first to arrive and the last to leave. They are responsible for locking up, checking that ovens, grills and lights are off and switching on alarm systems."

While many of these employees come up through the ranks of food service, a bachelor's degree in restaurant and food service management "provides a particularly strong preparation for a career in this occupation," according to the Department of Labor. This career group is expected to increase faster than the average for all occupations in the future.

The Specialty Professionals

The Department of Labor also provides projections for what it terms "Professional Specialty Occupations." These differ from the "Executive, Administrative, and Managerial Occupations" listed in the first section in that there are no managerial or administrative functions intrinsic to being in a "professional specialty occupation."

Engineers

The principles of math and science are the specialties of the engineers. They use these principles to solve practical technical problems economically. They transform scientific discoveries into products and services we can buy.

If a student decides to go into engineering he or she also must decide on an area of specialization: aerospace, chemical, civil, electrical and electronics, industrial, mechanical, metallurgical, ceramic and materials, mining, nuclear, petroleum, architectural, biomedical, environmental, and marine. Most engineers have a bachelor's degree, but many students choose to earn a degree from a technical college requiring a two- or four-year program of study. Employment is expected to increase about as fast as the average in this field.

Architects

All buildings start with a design that incorporates appearance, function, safety, and economy. Skills needed to accomplish this are design, engineering, managerial communication, and supervision.

Besides training in the field, a license is required for the architect in charge of a project. Graduates of architecture schools may work, but without a license they cannot be the architect who assumes legal responsibility for a project. Most architecture degrees are from five-year Bachelor of Architecture programs.

To obtain a license, a person needs 1) a professional degree in architecture, 2) a period of practical training or internship, usually for three years, 3) to pass all sections of the Architect Registration Examination.

Getting a job in this field depends heavily on the level of local construction. Many variables will affect job availability: urban renovation, needs of the under-15 and the over-65 age groups, or an anticipated slowdown in new construction. Still, employment growth of architects is expected to increase as fast as the average for all occupations.

This is not true for landscape architects, those people who design attractive residential areas, public parks, college campuses, shopping centers, golf courses, parkways, and industrial parks. The Department of Labor projects the number of openings to be too few to absorb all job seekers, because the number of degrees awarded has been steady even during times of fluctuating demand due to economic conditions.

Systems Analysts and Computer Scientists

"He or she works in computers," is a catchall phrase indicating that this field has grown faster than people can describe. The most often-used job category title is the systems analyst, those people who solve problems, figuring out how to make computer technology meet the needs of an organization.

According to the Department of Labor, these people "study business, scientific, or engineering data processing problems and design new solutions using computers. This process may include planning and developing new computer systems or devising ways to apply existing systems to operations still completed manually or by a less efficient method."

The systems analyst is a person who is able to concentrate, think logically, and be comfortable communicating with people and developing ideas in a team setting. Systems analysts must be detail oriented because technology is exacting. They also are people who continually need to update their information sources as technology rushes ahead.

Computer scientists work at a higher level of theoretical expertise and innovation than other professionals working in the computer industry. They create new technology and find applications. The category includes computer engineers, database administrators, computer support analysts, and a variety of other specialized workers.

If systems analysts work in an academic environment they have a range of opportunities from theory to hardware to language design. Those who work on interdisciplinary projects may develop and find uses for virtual reality technology.

Computer engineers are involved in both the hardware and software aspects of systems design and development. Frequently, they are part of a team that designs new computing devices or computer-related equipment.

The software of the database management systems is the area where the database administrators work. The Department of Labor states that they reorganize and restructure data to better suit the needs of users. They may also be responsible for maintaining the efficiency of the database, system security, and may implement design.

Computer support analysts answer the phones at the "help line." They interpret problems and provide technical support for hardware, software, and systems.

The Department of Labor sees a rosy picture for these experts, predicting these to be the among the fastest-growing occupations through the year 2005. An information explosion is in progress, with computer experts facilitating the sharing of this valuable commodity.

Foresters and Conservation Scientists

Visions of riding on horseback among hundred-year-old pines and thinking about nature is only one side of the options available as a forester. Those who work in industry may be responsible for buying timber from private landowners, which involves getting permission from the landowner to take inventory, appraise the timber, and negotiate a price. Next, they hire loggers to remove the trees, secure road layout, and continue communication with the buyer and seller to make sure the process is running smoothly. They must also comply with environmental regulations. Because environmental issues have high impact on natural resources, foresters consider how to conserve wildlife habitats, creek beds, water quality, and soil stability. In a process called *regeneration* they supervise the planting and growing of new trees and monitor the trees' growth.

Conservation scientists oversee the protection of rangeland and soil. Rangelands cover about 1 billion acres of the United States, mostly in the western states and Alaska, according to the Department of Labor. The soil and ranges contain many natural resources that need to be protected, such as grass and shrubs for animal grazing and watersheds.

Foresters and conservation scientists are called on to fight fires and to prevent erosion after a forest fire. They provide emergency help after floods, mudslides, and tropical storms. Some work in the national forests and parks, educating visitors about the necessity to conserve resources.

The job outlook for these picturesque experts is excellent, with their employment projected to grow as fast as the average for all occupations through the year 2005.

Chemists   Car oil, stay-on lipstick, and skin-like condoms are realities because of the chemists, a group of professionals who have studied physical things in the universe and converted them to practical uses. According to the Department of Labor, all physical things, whether naturally occurring or of human design, are composed of chemicals. In their laboratories chemists do research and development, but they also work in production and quality control in chemical manufacturing plants.

A demand for new and better pharmaceuticals and personal care products presents a promising employment picture for chemists. This occupation is expected to grow about as fast as the average for all occupations through 2005.

Lawyers   Although you hear that we have too many lawyers, the projections for this specialty are good. As a dean at Loyola University Law School said, "Ninety percent of the lawyers today are serving 10 percent of the people. If you think we have too many lawyers, sit in court one day and see what happens to people who are not represented by a lawyer." Lawyers are primarily researchers. Today, they are greatly aided by software programs that identify legal texts relevant to a specific case.

Most lawyers work in an area of specialization, such as trial work, taxes, real estate, bankruptcy, probate, environment, or international law. An emerging field is intellectual property, in which a lawyer helps protect clients' claim to copyrights, art work under contract, product designs, and computer programs. Lawyers in private practice usually concentrate on criminal or civil law. People charged with crimes are defended in court by criminal lawyers. Civil law involves litigation, wills, trusts, contracts, mortgages, titles, and leases.

Some lawyers work for a single client, or a corporation, where they are called "house counsel." All parts of government use lawyers to defend statutes and individuals, and to draft laws, interpret legislation, and argue cases for the government.

This occupation is expected to grow faster than average in the coming years, but competition will be fierce.

Social Scientists

Social scientists study people and what they do. They conduct surveys, interviews, field investigations, laboratory experiments, and standardized tests and interpret maps and computer graphics. Through the results of their research, people are better able to make decisions, exercise power, or respond to change.

Within this category are several subgroups:

Anthropologists study what has happened to the human race culturally, socially, linguistically, and physically as far back as they can determine.

Geographers look at the distribution of physical and cultural phenomena locally, regionally, continentally, and globally. This may involve looking at the distribution of resources and economic activity, or health care delivery systems.

Historians look at the past to find wisdom for the future. They are usually specialists, looking at a particular time, a country or region, or in a particular field, such as intellectual history.

Political scientists look at political systems, such as the Republican or Democratic party, or at public policy, such as capital punishment.

Psychologists constitute more than half of the social

scientist group and study human behavior and give advice to individuals or groups. They are sometimes confused with psychiatrists, a group of people with medical degrees who can prescribe drugs.

Sociologists study the behavior of groups of people and how these groups interact. They study the effect of social traits, such as sex, age, or race, on a person's daily life.

Urban and regional planners look at population growth and make suggestions for the best use of land. They are also concerned with social and economic change and how these affect future plans.

Students choosing one of these fields can expect faster-than-the-average growth in employment.

Economists and Marketing Research Analysts

Economists collect data on the way society distributes scarce resources such as land, labor, raw materials, and machinery to produce goods and services. They are frequently quoted in the media with projections for trends and spending. They are researchers, using surveys, mathematical models, surveys, and charts. Business and industry use their expertise in making plans for production and sales.

Those who work for the government estimate the economic effects of specific changes in legislation or public policy.

Marketing research analysts gather information on sales, preferences of consumers, and past patterns of consumption. Sugar-coated cereals sold well in the past, but will health consciousness damper their sales in the future? These are the sorts of questions they are assigned to research. Once they have collected data through questionnaires, surveys, and interviews, they compile their results and make recommendations to management of companies about the sale of their products.

The employment of both economists and marketing research analysts is expected to grow faster than average for all occupations.

Social Workers

The world's problems fall at the door of the social worker, who is there to help people cope with whatever problems they are facing. This might be mental illness, unemployment, inadequate housing, financial mismanagement, serious illness, disability, substance abuse, unwanted pregnancy, antisocial behavior, or abuse. Often, they have concrete information on where help can be found. Or they may listen and help identify concerns, consider solutions, and find resources. Like lawyers, they have specialties such as child welfare or family services, protective services, mental health, health care, school social work, criminal justice, occupations, gerontology, and policy and planning. The aging of the population, the rise of crime, and rising concern for the mentally and physically sick will increase the employment of these professionals faster than the average for all occupations, according to the Department of Labor.

Clergy and Rabbis

Now is a good time to become a Catholic priest or a rabbi, but not such a good time to consider being a Protestant minister, according to the Department of Labor. If you are a woman, it is still impossible to become a Catholic priest, and women may not become clergy in some Protestant denominations either. As priests retire, die, or leave the priesthood it has been increasingly difficult to fill their shoes. So the job outlook for them is expected to be very favorable.

Adult Education Teachers

Free of spitballs and the-dog-ate-my-homework excuses, teachers who educate adults have many advantages. They work in an environment of highly motivated people who are in the classroom by choice. About half of them work part time, and many have other jobs. Because the group in the 35 to 44 age range, the largest users of adult education, is expected to expand, the rate of job growth is expected to be faster than the average.

College and University Faculty

While most students feel they know what faculty do, the reality is quite different. Besides teaching, they conduct research, write, address conferences in their fields with their latest findings, attend academic or administrative committee meetings, and counsel individual students on academic problems. They accomplish these tasks in addition to preparing lectures, often to be delivered to hundreds of students, grading papers, and writing exams.

Employment of college and university faculty is expected to increase about as fast as the average for all occupations, according to the Department of Labor. The Department predicts that retirements of the faculty that was hired in the 1950s and 1960s will produce employment opportunities.

Teachers   Job outlooks for special education teachers, who work with students, from toddlers to those in their early 20s, who have a variety of disabilities, are excellent. But the geography of where these people are needed is tricky, mostly in rural areas and the inner cities. The job market for other teachers varies widely depending on geographic area. The Department of Labor states that teachers in math, science, bilingual education, and computer science are in short supply. Others, those in elementary education, physical education, and social studies, are in oversupply.

Chiropractors   Chiropractors take care of the spine and the body's muscular, nervous, and skeletal systems. They stress the patient's overall well-being and emphasize proper eating, exercise, and sleeping patterns. They order diagnostic tests and use spinal and postural analysis to recommend a course of treatment, which does not use drugs or surgery but manipulation or adjustment of the spinal column. The employment of these holistic practitioners is expected to grow faster than the average as the profession continues to grow in acceptance and public awareness and as the population ages.

Optometrists   Optometrists deal with the eyes and shouldn't be confused with ophthalmologists or opticians. Ophthalmologists are physicians who diagnose and treat the eyes. They also examine eyes and prescribe eyeglasses. They perform surgery and write prescriptions. Opticians fit and adjust eyeglasses and are allowed in some states to fit contact lenses. Optometrists examine eyes, treat eye disease, prescribe eyeglasses and contact lenses, and develop treatment plans.

In response to the growth of the aging population, jobs for optometrists should grow about as fast as the average. The Baby Boomers will provide work as they reach 45, the onset of vision problems in middle age.

Physicians   Students who want to become physicians have two concerns to consider: 1) it takes eleven years: four years of college, four years of medical school, and three years in residency, and 2) some health care analysts believe that there soon could be a general oversupply of doctors. Others disagree.

Job prospects are favorable for generalists, such as primary care physicians, family practitioners, and internists and for geriatric and preventive care specialists. Other specialty areas have been handicapped because of efforts to control health care costs and guidelines that limit the use of specialists.

Podiatrists

While many people rely on "Dr. Scholl" to alleviate minor foot pain, even more turn to licensed foot doctors, or podiatrists, to treat serious disorders, diseases, and injuries to the feet and lower legs. Podiatrists can prescribe drugs, order physical therapy, set fractures, and perform surgery. Most are solo practitioners or have private practices, but the Department of Labor finds that more and more are entering partnerships and multispecialty group practices. Employment of podiatrists is expected to grow about as fast as the average for all occupations through the year 2005 due to an aging population that will depend on foot care. However, the amount of disposable income available to the patients may affect the number of people seeking foot care, since only acute medical and surgical foot care is covered by most insurance plans. Routine foot care must be paid for out-of-pocket.

Veterinarians

In an age of pet weddings and wardrobes, it's hardly surprising that the job outlook for veterinarians is good. The same people who treat their cats and dogs to toys and clothing have shown a not surprising willingness to pay for intensive medical care for their pets. Although the majority of veterinarians specialize in treating small companion animals, others treat livestock, sporting, and laboratory animals, and even protect humans against animal-borne diseases. Veterinarians can also work in zoos and aquariums, in food safety inspection, and in animal research. A good veterinarian has the ability to calm animals, get along with pet owners, and make emergency decisions. Employment of veterinarians is expected to grow about as fast as the average, and better for those with specialty training in toxicology, laboratory animal medicine, animal behavior, or pathology.

Dietitians and Nutritionists

The word *diet* connotes the practice of restricting a person's food intake to promote weight loss. But dieticians plan nutrition programs and supervise the preparation and serving of food for all people. The Department of Labor defines four major areas of practice: clinical, community, management, and consultant dietetics. Clinical dieticians provide nutritional services for patients in institutions such as hospitals and nursing homes. Community dieticians counsel individuals and groups on nutritional practices designed to prevent disease and promote good health. Management dieticians oversee large-scale meal planning and preparation in such places as health care facilities, company cafeterias, prisons, and schools. Consultant dieticians work with clients under contract with health care facilities or in their own private practices. Employment of dieticians is expected to grow at the average rate due to increased awareness of the importance of eating healthful foods in the prevention of certain diseases. Growth may be hindered, however, by the substitutability of other workers (nurses, health educators, etc.) for dieticians and limitations on insurance reimbursement for dietetic services.

Occupational Therapists

Some occupational therapists do exactly what their name suggests: help people find and hold a job. But the people they often help have physical, mental, emotional, or developmental disabilities that make daily tasks and job performance difficult. Other occupational therapists work with patients to develop and maintain living skills, which sometimes involves designing and making special equipment needed for patients' homes or jobs. Prospective occupational therapists should be comfortable treating disabled people with the patience and ingenuity it often demands. Students interested in pursuing a career in occupational therapy should have excellent grades because most four-year programs are highly competitive. Job opportunities for occupational therapists are expected to grow much faster than the average for all other jobs through the year 2005 due to an anticipated growth in demand for rehabilitation and long-term care services.

Pharmacists

Physicians prescribe drugs; pharmacists are needed to fill the prescriptions and provide important information about medications and their uses. Pharmacists work with doctors, advising them on the selection, dosages, interactions, and side effects of medications. Hospital pharmacists often advance to directors of pharmacy services or other administrative positions, and those in the pharmaceutical industry can advance in the marketing, sales, research, quality control, production, and packaging of medications. Employment of pharmacists is expected to grow at an average rate, hindered only by the use of automated dispensing systems in pharmacies, and the rising enrollment at colleges of pharmacy, both contributing to higher competition.

Physical Therapists

Physical therapists use a variety of innovative tools and practices to treat patients suffering from injuries or disease. Treatments often include exercise, electrical stimulation, hot or cold compresses, and even deep-tissue massages. Physical therapists treat a wide range of patients, from those suffering broken limbs to those recovering from heart attacks. Some physical therapists work in all areas, while others specialize in areas such as pediatrics, geriatrics, orthopaedics, sports medicine, neurology, and cardiopulmonary therapy. Physical therapy programs at most schools have very competitive entry requirements, so students interested are advised to work for outstanding grades in high school and in the first two years of general college study. The reward for the hard work is the many job offers a physical therapy graduate is likely to receive. Physical therapy is expected to be one of the fastest-growing occupations through the year 2005, according to the Department of Labor.

Recreational Therapists

Like occupational therapists, recreational therapists work with disabled patients. But unlike occupational therapists, who help patients with functional activities, recreational therapists treat or maintain the physical, mental, and emotional well-being of their patients by designing sports, games, dance, drama, arts and crafts, and music, as well as field trips for sightseeing, ball games, and picnics. In the clinical setting, recreational therapists work with physicians, nurses, psychologists, social workers, and other therapists to treat patients with specific medical problems. In community-based programs, such as park and recreational departments, special education programs, or programs for the elderly or disabled, they help patients develop leisure activities, provide them with the opportunities to do what they like and have fun. The occupation is growing at a faster rate than average because of anticipated expansion in long-term care, physical and psychiatric rehabilitation, and services for the disabled.

Writers and Editors

A collaboration exists behind every book, magazine, newspaper, movie, radio or television program, or advertisement: the writer and the editor. Writers select and organize material and put it into words that effectively convey the information to the reader. Editors then review, rewrite, and edit the work of writers. An editor's primary job, however, is to plan the material content and supervise production processes. Most writers and editors work for newspapers, magazines, and book publishers, although many work in advertising, radio and television, public relations, and on journals or newsletters published by businesses and nonprofit organizations. Technical writers, who make scientific and technical information easily understandable to a nontechnical audience, work for computer software firms or manufacturers of chemical, pharmaceutical, and electronic manufacturers. The Department of Labor expects employment of writers and editors to increase faster than the average of all other occupations through 2005. Many opportunities will open as a result of a high turnover rate in this profession.

Designers

Everything in daily use—cars, houses, offices, appliances, computers, clothing, newspapers, even flower arrangements—is designed by professionals who know what is functional and pleasing to the eye as well. Designers constantly search for new ways to make things better by determining needs and weighing factors such as ease of use, safety, and cost efficiency. Design encompasses many diverse fields, but all have one thing in common: talented experts. Most fields demand formal training in each design field as well as aptitude in computers and the latest in technology. Employment, though competitive, is expected to grow at a faster rate than average through 2005.

Actors, Directors and Producers

These professionals are devoted to expressing ideas, creating images, and stirring emotions in an audience. Actors communicate their interpretations of dramatic roles, directors interpret plays or scripts to decide what themes or major ideas are to be presented, and producers select plays or scripts they then finance and budget. Formal dramatic training or theater experience is generally necessary, but some actors have successfully entered the field without it. There are no specific requirements for directors and producers, but talent, experience, and business knowledge are important. Employment of actors, directors, and producers is expected to grow faster than the average of all other occupations. However, this field may be affected by government funding for the arts—a decline in funding could dampen interests in this field.

Clinical Laboratory Technologists and Technicians

The process of detecting, diagnosing, and treating a disease often begins in clinical laboratories where technicians examine and analyze body fluids, tissues, and cells. They search for bacteria, analyze the content of fluids, match blood for transfusions, and test for drug levels in the blood to see how a person is responding to medical treatment. The complexity of tests performed, the level of judgment needed, and the amount of responsibility workers assume depend largely on the amount of education and experience they have. Most jobs in clinical laboratory technology require a bachelor's degree in medical technology or life science, although some require only an associate's degree, and others require just experience. (After September 1, 1997, the Clinical Laboratory Improvement Act (CLIA) requires technologists who perform certain highly complex tests to have at least an associate's degree.) Employment of clinical laboratory technicians is expected to grow at the average rate, hindered only by advances in laboratory automation and simpler tests, which make it possible for each worker to perform more tests.

Nuclear Medicine Technologists

Nuclear medicine has revolutionized the way disease can be detected and diagnosed. By injecting radionuclides or unstable atoms that emit radiation spontaneously into a patient, nuclear medicine technologists can then track the radioactive drug as it appears in the body and capture the images on photographic film. This procedure is useful in bone scans to detect abnormalities, in cardiac function studies, and in determining blood-hormone levels. Nuclear medicine technology programs range from one to four years and lead to certificates, associate or bachelor degrees. Job prospects for nuclear medicine technologists are expected to be good. The number of job openings per year, however, will be low because the occupation is very small. Some promising nuclear medicine procedures are extremely costly, and many hospitals are still contemplating the equipment costs, reimbursement policies, and the number of potential users. But overall, according to the Department of Labor, the employment of nuclear medicine technologists is expected to grow faster than the average for all occupations through the year 2005.

Computer Programmers

These professionals should not be confused with the systems analyst, computer scientist, computer engineer, database administrator, or computer support analyst described earlier. The computer programmer performs several duties including following the descriptions prepared by systems analysts who have studied the task. Others do both jobs as one. Obviously, this occupation requires a strong aptitude for computers and changes in technology. But one changing requirement is the level of education. For years, training, a certificate, or an associate degree were sufficient to enter the field of computer programming. But bachelor's degrees are now commonly required. Employment is expected to grow at the average rate of all other occupations.

Paralegals

Paralegals do everything that lawyers do, except practice law. They assist with background work, investigate facts of cases, gather all relevant information, conduct research on past cases, and analyze and organize all the information. Several types of paralegal training programs are acceptable to enter the field, but increasingly, employers prefer to hire either graduates of four-year paralegal programs or those with bachelor's degrees who have earned paralegal certificates through short-term programs after graduation. Employment of paralegals is expected to grow much faster than the average for all occupations through the year 2005.

Learning from Others: Real People Talk About Their Majors

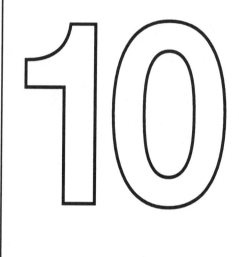

10

Philosophies differ on what a college education should be. Having a good time for four years is a popular notion. Others, witnessing harsh economic readjustment over the past few years, believe college should prepare you for a job. The traditional belief is that college is a time to grow, to broaden your awareness. In the following comments, many former and current students have offered their opinions on what a major means and how the one they chose affects their lives today.

Jamie Wirt,
Roosevelt University,
B.A. 1990
Majors: Music,
History

Music is my area of life. I work in music and play in music. I fell into a history major by taking many history courses, and by just taking a few more, I earned a major. I did, although, enjoy the classes and even received an award in history.

I am now a producer, an engineer, and a musician. I

tour as a musician, record records as an engineer, and produce toys and records as a producer.

The best part of my job is being in music and doing something different every day. The worst part is not knowing for sure if I will get a paycheck next week. This is because I am self-employed.

My music major gave me several skills that relate directly to my current jobs, such as my aural and voice training in discerning pitch and musical nuance. I also learned valuable tools that I use as a producer, things like song structure and harmonic content. Some skills, like intensive computer and technical skills, I gained through experience in the studio.

If I had it to do all over again, I would have chosen a school where the composition teachers would have done more to lead me in interesting and pertinent directions. The best advice I can give is to get a degree in a well-rounded area, i.e., Bachelor of Arts. Don't worry so much about job skills as related to a major, just get a general degree to open your mind to what life has to offer, and then you can proceed from there.

Scott Minafri, Glassboro State College, B.S. 1992 Major: Management Information Systems (MIS)

I've always had a knack for computing, but I didn't want to be completely technical, like computer science. MIS gave me an opportunity to be exposed to the management side of things as well as the technical.

My job title is network manager—I was just promoted in August. Basically, I manage the local area network and handle PC support for the finance division. This encompasses about twenty file servers, and about 450 users. I have three systems administrators working for me. The worst part of my job is the hours—they can sometimes be a little crazy. The best part is being able to work with the new technology immediately once it becomes available.

My major, unfortunately, does not relate much to my current job. MIS is a lot of theory, not practice. Being an MIS major helped with my managerial skills, but that's about it. The one thing that college was good for is that it taught me how to think. My job requires a strong aptitude for computer systems, the ability to be resourceful, and the ability to take initiative.

The best advice I can give students is to find something you really enjoy, and go with it. If you're unsure, then just pick something and concentrate on graduating. Once you're out of school, it's a whole different ballgame.

John Swazey,
University of
California, San
Diego, B.A. 1990
Major: Chemistry;
Minor: Performance
Theater

I had a natural knack at chemistry. I very much enjoyed the classes, the assignments, and even taking the tests, especially during the first year of lower-division classes.

I am currently a staff chemist for Oilfield Applications Research and Development. I have held this job with one promotion in title for just under six years. The best part of my job is designing and running experiments to investigate things. The worst part is the writing (reports, lab notebooks, etc.).

My degree in chemistry relates to my job in a very general way. It helped me to know how to approach problem solving and to apply general principles. It also taught me basic laboratory skills, and helped me to express myself effectively in writing. My job requires creativity, good observation skills, laboratory skills, computer and writing skills.

Approach college with a thirst for knowledge rather than a thirst for a good grade. Pick a major that you enjoy; one that challenges you but that you find you have a knack for and enjoy being challenged at.

Daniel Dutile,
University of
Notre Dame, B.S. 1987
Major: Business
Administration/
Finance
MBA: University of
Chicago

It really was a process of elimination for me. I knew I wanted something in business. Marketing, management, and accounting were not really to my liking, however. Finance was left as the choice offering me enough business focus, with enough flexibility of curriculum.

I have been an equity portfolio manager for eight months. I am responsible for deciding where a portion of a large corporate retirement plan's assets should be invested. The best part of my job is making sense of the actions of the stock markets around the world. The worst part is dealing with the frustration when the stock markets' movements defy analysis.

As a finance major, I was exposed to the basic theories that tend to govern financial markets. I utilize this knowledge to analyze the markets in which we invest. My job requires skills in financial analysis, decision making, communication of ideas, and personnel management.

I underestimated the importance of accounting skills in my career and in financial analysis in general. If I had it to do all over again, I would improve these skills.

The best advice I can give students is to choose a major that you enjoy. Competence will show itself in whatever major is chosen. The future will then take care of itself.

***Deborah Prince,
University of Iowa,
B.S. 1995
Major: Therapeutic
Recreation***

I have been a certified recreational therapist for three months. I assess patients according to their disabilities and interests, adapt activities that enable them to do the things they want to do, and help them as much as possible. The best part of my job is working with and getting to know each patient on an individual basis. The worst is the same as the best—knowing and caring about the patients. It's hard not to get personally involved, and when they leave or pass away, it is very difficult.

My major relates exactly to what I do now. I learned how to document and assess patients with disabilities in school.

My job requires the ability to relate to people who are sick, and strong documentation skills. Honestly, I wouldn't change a thing if I had to go back. I feel being able to do something for someone else is very rewarding. I would advise students to choose a field that you know you can wake up in the morning and be enthusiastic about. Recreational therapy allows me to do just that.

***Gregory Fung,
Harvard College,
B.S. 1995
Major: Biochemistry***

I chose this major because when I first entered college, I felt fairly certain that I would either go into medicine or biomedical research. As far as I could tell, this major provided the best opportunities for both of those fields.

I am currently a volunteer staff worker for InterVarsity Christian Fellowship, having just started two months ago after spending a year working with urban squatters in the Philippines. My job consists of helping lead a college Christian fellowship, including leading Bible studies, teaching during leadership training times, organizing retreats and other events, pastoring students, and other related activities.

The best part of the job is being able to take part, see, and contribute to students' spiritual, mental, and emotional growth. The worst part is in feeling (and note that these feelings are not necessarily true) that the job is pointless, unproductive, hurtful to my future, and degrading.

My college major has almost nothing to do with what I do now, except that I can relate well with students who are in the same biochemistry or premed track that I was on. My job requires (in order of importance): counseling skills, teaching skills, leadership/ administration, good speaking or musical skills, depending on the specific ministry one is in.

If I could do it all over again, I would not major in biochemistry. I would probably have done something in the social sciences like sociology, psychology, or anthropology. I might even have gone the philosophy route. The core of the choice would be to go for a more broad and more socially relevant major, rather than a narrower and skill-focused field (assuming that I would know that I would not end up in medicine).

I would say that you need not rush to make a decision concerning a major, nor feel like you need to stick to the decision once made. I would also say that certain "career" majors such as biology should only be chosen if you think that you could do nothing else. Even if you end up going into biology, you can wait to fulfill the major requirements and take other classes so you don't lose out on the unique things a college education can offer.

Erin Shean, University of San Diego, B.A. 1987 Major: Communication Studies; Minor: Legal Studies

I thought that I wanted to attend law school after college and believed that communications would be a good background, and I enjoyed those classes the most. I have been a paralegal for six years. I assist attorneys in case management and preparation for trial and do some investigative work.

The best part of my job is the interaction with clients. The worst is the pay. My job requires the skills of organization, investigation, writing, and communication. My minor has more relevance to my career than my major does. The basic principles of communication, however, are used every day in this profession.

If I had it to do all over again, I would have either gone directly into law school after college or I would have chosen another career. The best advice I can give is to speak to a career counselor and take a career inventory survey that lists your strengths and weaknesses and which professions you would be best suited for with those strengths.

Alexandra Wray, Cornell University, B.A. 1996 Major: Art and Architecture

Cornell offered a five-year program that gave me a bachelor's degree in architecture, as opposed to just a major. It is a professional degree, and the training for architecture is well-rounded, so even if I choose not to be an architect, I have a good education.

I am an architect at a firm in downtown Chicago. I have been there for just over two months. I assist a team, do Autocad work, build models, render, whatever they need. The variety of tasks is the best part of the job—they are creative. I don't just collate photocopies all day. It is, however, stressful and it invades my life. Deadlines, deadlines, deadlines. School was what we liked to call playland. In school we honed our problem-solving skills and design theory. The profession, however, is very into precision, cost, client, efficiency. In some ways we are prepared well in terms of thought and endurance, but we never studied in-depth fire protection, code, etc. I am learning every day at work. My job requires neatness. I must produce architectural models quickly, but make them as perfect as possible. Rendering drawings, Autocad are very important skills.

If I had it to do all over again, I would win the lottery! Just kidding. To support myself with this profession will be very tough. But I don't think being an investment banker would be nearly as interesting.

When choosing a major, you have to think, What interests me? You also have to look at the big picture. Don't take easy ways out to make college more fun. Consider time—you don't have forever. Hard work is rewarding. Research careers, fields, and what lifestyle they typically entail.

Lara Rhame, Bates College, B.A. 1993 Major: Economics

It was the end of my sophomore year, and I needed to choose. So I thought economics or psychology were the best mix of practical and interesting, and I went to talk to professors in each department. The econ professors were much more impressive. I was taking both at the time, and I really liked economics better.

I have been a risk manager for two years. I evaluate portfolio, credit, and market risk on the trading floor at Lehman Brothers. The best part of my job is learning every day about the markets and being in the center of the international financial world. The worst are the egocentric, mean, self-centered, ultracapitalistic traders and salespeople you have to deal with.

My major doesn't relate especially well to my job, except for the way economic factors could influence the market. But they are definitely in the same arena, with a lot of overlapping (especially the math classes I had to take).

My job requires quick thinking, the gift of gab, the ability to learn on the fly, computer and financial skills, statistics and math skills.

I am a fan of liberal arts, but I was careful to choose a major I thought would be practical. For example, I was very interested in Japanese art and religions, and thought about double majoring in Asian culture. In the end, it would have been overkill. But now I have it as a hobby, and still follow it passionately. This is not to say to major in something you abhor, just for practical reasons, but really think it through. There is a difference between thinking something is cool and wanting to center your college experience around it.

Margaret Wuebbels, Southern Methodist University, B.A. 1990 Majors: Psychology, History; Minor: Women's Studies University of Arizona Law School, 1994

I was interested in becoming a psychologist at one point. I also had an interest in law and I thought history would be helpful, as would psychology.

I have been an attorney for two years. I am a trial lawyer and a public defender. I represent criminally indigent people. The best part of my job is being in court. The worst is the frustration with "the system."

My majors both required lots of writing. My background in psychology is helpful in selecting juries and dealing with people: other attorneys, reluctant witnesses, and clients. History gave me an overall intellectual view of law in American history.

My job requires the ability to speak in public and argue a case in court. It also demands the ability to negotiate and write clearly.

I would do nothing differently if given the chance. I waited three semesters to pick a major and really explored my options. Shop around. Study something you enjoy because you'll never get to do it again. Virtually any major can get you any job.

Natalie Melnik, University of Pittsburgh, B.A. 1995 Major: Sociology; Minor: French

I am an international sales coordinator for Anixter Inc. I provide consultations and various sales support to the U.S.-based salespeople at my company, as well as the foreign. The best part of my job is working with people. The worst part of my job is working with people.

My major helped me develop people skills, an understanding of the psychology of the business environment, statistics skills, demography, intercultural understanding, and computer skills. My job requires all of these skills, plus communications skills and a mentality to get the job done.

I would not change a thing. I still love my major. I was never disappointed once in four years. It's very multifaceted. I would advise students to match their genuine interests with the college programs and course offerings.

Sarah Kennedy,
Loyola University,
B.A. 1995
Major: Sociology;
Minor: Social Work

I originally chose social work as a major, but switched because it only focused on the person as the problem and not necessarily the system. Sociology focused more on the system and how to create change in this area. I enjoyed sociology much more. I am the associate director for a nonprofit agency working with teenagers. We have programs in public schools and the surrounding communities of the specific schools. The programs use peer-to-peer interventions to help stop violence. It is an agency committed to working with at-risk economically poor young adults to motivate them into becoming more responsible. The best part of the job, working with teens, is also the most challenging, but I do enjoy it. The worst is seeing peer pressure and gangs and to deal with death, abuse, neglect, and lack of values.

I'm in the social service field, so my major has helped me understand more systematically what's going on. For example, I must look at one teen's behavior and discover why she is acting this way. Sociology helped me to do this. Someone who is abused may act out in many ways, or someone who is very overweight may have had many problems in his past. We must look at people's behavior, but don't judge, accept it and challenge them to become more positive. My job requires me to work with people. It requires skills of facilitating, conflict management, and the ability to implement change.

If I had it to do all over again, I might go to school later and study more. I wish I had taken school more seriously. I think some Americans don't appreciate school for what it's worth. The best advice I can think of is to talk to other students, teachers, and counselors, but don't think you can't change majors—you can. There are many resources one can use to learn more about majors. Honestly, I don't think a major is that important unless it's a technical one (i.e., math, computers, science).

Robert Gibson,
Bowling Green State
University, B.S. 1986
Major: Visual
Communication
Technology (VCT)

VCT (graphics) was an area I had some interest and ability in, and it was a less threatening avenue to pursue and still be in a communications field. I figured I could go into advertising and still be on the fringes of a glamorous career, instead of going directly into theater or film (too competitive, too scary). It was also a "hands-on" field; one that would give me hard skills that I could market and sell for quick employment.

I am currently a graduate student at Loyola University

Chicago pursuing a M.Ed. in college student personnel. My last professional position was as a university admissions and recruitment counselor. The best part of any job I've had is having something to get out of bed for and supporting my own existence. The worst is feeling like I have to determine my success, image, and happiness by my job title and salary due to the American societal imposition (achieving the "American Dream").

My major had nothing to do with my jobs. My jobs have all required moxie—fearlessness and perseverence (qualities I don't always possess), written and oral communications skills, which incorporate diplomacy and tact, organizational abilities, and focus.

If I could go back in time, I would have chosen a different major, theater or popular culture, because I don't believe the major is the most important aspect of anyone's education. My VCT major was very task oriented, which did not teach me anything about moxie.

I would give this advice to students choosing a college major: don't panic! Academically, concentrate on general education requirements and, in the meantime, research the career area(s) you are interested in to determine if you would really be satisfied with that/those choice(s) in the long run. This research includes volunteer work, internships/co-ops, and extracurriculars. Do things to build personal skills (communication, organization, leadership). There will always be time to choose a major that most of the general education classes will satisfy. That way, you won't be facing your final year of study feeling trapped in a field that you've discovered you can't stand, which will also lead to less career instability. You may find yourself less susceptible to a mid-life career switch and the feeling of having to start all over again.

*Larissa Zoot,
University of
Wisconsin at
LaCrosse, 1992
Major: Community
Health Education*

LaCrosse is well known for health and fitness programs. I started out in sports management, but by the end of my first semester, I was so impressed and motivated by the health education faculty that I wanted to be like them, so I switched. I'm currently in the second and final year of a Masters in Public Health program in health management and policy at the University of Michigan. And I'm starting to look for a job for when I'm done. I'm really interested in doing more health/development work in other countries, so I'm mostly looking at international fellowships and the like. The best part is that I'm learning a lot of valuable information about how the health care system works, how resources are allocated, etc. And I have great friends here who are a wonderful support system during school and will be a great network of professional colleagues when I'm done. The worst is that grad school is hard work, and quite overwhelming at times. It can be really exhausting, and you have to be really motivated to get through it. (Oh, and it's costing a fortune. I'll be in debt for years!) I've pretty much been in health subjects throughout school and in all of my work experiences during and in between undergraduate and graduate school. I have shifted focus with each experience, though. For example, as an undergrad I focused on sexually transmitted diseases and decision-making issues. In one internship I focused on parenting skills, and in another I focused on training public health workers. In the Peace Corps I focused on maternal and child health, so it's all health, but it's all over the map. I'm trying to get a broad base of experience so then I can settle down and choose what I really like and care about.

As far as the Peace Corps, I had many reasons for doing it, but two especially stand out in my mind. I was intrigued by the idea that I could live at a lower standard of living while at the same time help others to develop a higher level of living. I also wanted to test my education and skills in a setting where I thought it would really matter to others. I wanted to get my hands in the dirt, not just sit behind a desk! I learned a lot by being there. I learned that there is order and balance in the world, that everything works out OK, that little inconveniences are not major obstacles, that little things and individual people are more significant than we tend to think they are, that I can handle just about anything that comes my way, that I am strong, adaptable, and that I have the ability to touch people's lives in meaningful ways and be touched by others through the simplest acts of kindness and friendship. If I had it to do all over again, I would have studied harder in high school. I didn't, and my grades were not at all in line with what I was capable of. If I hadn't gotten high test scores, I might not have even gotten into a decent college.

The best advice I can give is not to be in a hurry to choose a major. Get a feel for several different things. And use the university's resources to help find out what your options are and where your talents lie. Also, don't feel trapped once you have chosen. I know lots of people who don't end up doing what they studied as an undergraduate. It's not like you are stuck with your decision forever.

Gemma Smith, Texas Christian University, B.A. 1987 Major: Radio, TV, & Film; Minor: Psychology

I chose my major for the most frivolous of reasons. I knew I wanted to be in communications, and there was this multiple choice question my first day of college. It said: 1) Journalism, 2) Advertising, or 3) Radio, TV, and Film. Check one. So I checked Radio, TV, and Film because I figured I might as well enjoy myself for the next four years. And I did.

I am an associate producer right now for two TV series on a cable network. I write, organize information, coordinate crews, manage budgets, and try to choose great shots when editing shows. The best part of my job is the excitement of the set and being on location. The tremendous challenge of creativity: something out of nothing. And the diversity of projects. The worst is the challenge of creativity: something great out of nothing. And the long hours.

My major relates to what I do in mostly superficial ways. Spending time in college learning the basics of production is silly in retrospect because I learned all my real production skills on the job. Technology changes so fast that the equipment I used in college just nine years ago is totally antiquated. Some classes on theory and the social impact and responsibility of the media were valuable to me in developing my perspective. As a whole, I think a journalism or English major would have been more beneficial to me because being a good writer is very important in television (although it might be hard to believe sometimes).

My job requires enthusiasm, endurance, written communication skills, and oral communication skills. In TV you must be able to explain your idea of shots and visual images to a lot of people. Being able to accurately communicate your vision for a project is critical. The inability to do this can cost you thousands of dollars and days of shooting. If I had it to do all over again, I would concentrate more on my writing skills. I would also take more speech classes to learn to project and to organize my thoughts. I would still minor in psychology, because understanding where people are coming from and their basic motivations is helpful no matter what you do. I sometimes wonder if my major would have been totally useless if I hadn't pursued a career in TV. But I know a lot of people with the same degree doing various unrelated things, and they are very successful. I think I made the right choice because I really enjoyed the classes in college and I really enjoy my work now. I could be a success doing a lot of things besides production. As a matter of fact, I am branching out into public relations and marketing. I am anxious to combine my production skills with new PR projects like corporate video, and this way I can continue doing video but have more of a 9 to 5 lifestyle.

I would advise students to choose a major that will give them broadly applicable, valuable skills such as English, business, speech, or management. Learn to think critically, write a sentence, understand people, balance a budget, etc. If you are very sure of what you want to do, still, don't choose a major targeted selectively at that field, even though it is tempting. Later on you might want to change careers, and you might be too limited. Instead, use your free time to volunteer in your field of interest, and get specific internships in that field. That practical experience will serve you better and impress employers more than a degree in a super-specific field.

Joe Sifferman, Texas A & M University, B.S. 1995 Major: Biomedical Engineering Industrial Engineering, M.S. 1996

I chose an engineering degree for several reasons not necessarily related to the specific content of the fields of study. An engineering degree would allow me to sharpen and refine my problem-solving abilities, it would allow me more freedom for job and career selection in the future, and it would be a challenge. I originally chose bioengineering because I had entertained thoughts of pursuing a career in the medical field. I ended up going into industrial engineering because it's a good all-around engineering degree. It has more emphasis on business concepts than other engineering disciplines. IE also provides a strong background in economic and statistical analysis.

I am currently an analyst for information technology for a management consulting firm. The best part of my job is the variety of work and the work environment. There are tremendous opportunities for learning, travel, and a potential for a future. The worst part is the long hours (50 to 60 hours a week). My job requires analytical thinking, problem solving, the ability to learn and adapt, and computer skills. I gained all of these skills through my majors. I would change nothing if given the opportunity.

The best advice I can give is choose something that interests you (that should be obvious), but that also provides the greatest potential (not necessarily monetary) for you and your future. I submit that most people in industry do not use their specific collegiate education knowledge in their everyday work. Therefore, I believe the most important things to get out of school are how to learn, exposure to various fields of study, basic core knowledge (writing skills, math/statistics skills, etc.), and exposure to diversity (cultures, ways of thinking, etc.).

Jeremy Benoit, Northern Illinois University, B.S. 1996 Major: Operations Management and Information Systems (OMIS)

I chose this major because I was getting good grades in the prebusiness classes for OMIS, I knew I would have a good job after graduation, there are a lot of growth opportunities in this field, and class materials got me interested in participation.

I have been a programmer/consultant since I graduated. I use my major emphasis in information systems by designing computer applications for users in my company to use to make their jobs easier. The best part of my job is the great salary and benefits. There are plenty of jobs available if I want to switch companies. It's a dynamic work environment. I can't think of anything bad about my chosen field.

I apply a lot of what I learned in class to what I do at work. Classes weren't as in-depth as experience on the job has proven, but were good in preparing me for a job in my field. My job requires creativity, common sense, professionalism in business, personality, and the ability to work in groups.

I wouldn't change much if I had it to do all over again. I got a good education at a reasonable price, even though NIU doesn't have a big name like Harvard or Yale. I would advise students to check your options early, maybe as a senior in high school. I know that's early to be thinking of something that is five years off, but trust me. It will pay off. Find out what you are good at (science, math, etc.), and find a major that will let your abilities be explored.

Catherine Berghoff, Northern Arizona University, B.S. 1990 Major: Communications; Minor: Business Grand Canyon University, M.A. 1995 Major: Education— English as a Second Language (ESL)

After I got my undergraduate degree, I realized I wanted to work with kids whose native language wasn't English. I've always enjoyed studying language, and education seemed to fit my needs. I'm an ESL teacher at the middle school level. I have taught here for four years. I teach six ESL math and bilingual classes a day. I'm also department chair for ESL and math. The best part of my job: I love working with kids, presenting them with new information and getting them excited to learn. The worst is the paperwork, and there are never enough hours in the day.

My undergraduate degree doesn't relate, except with the people skills I acquired. My master's degree relates because it's so specified—linguistics and working with children learning two languages, how to best teach them, and assess them as well. My job requires the skills of planning, organization, patience, and people skills (you have to be approachable).

If I could do it all over again, I would have studied education in my undergraduate years and listened more to myself and what I wanted to do as opposed to peers and family pressure to pursue a career that didn't really suit me.

The best advice for students choosing a major is to think about how each major will prepare you for the work environment. It should be something you feel strongly about, but also practical and applicable to the real world.

Kristofer Arthur, University of Illinois at Chicago, B.S. 1996 Major: Information Design Systems (IDS)

I chose IDS because of my love for systems design and the good job market for computer-related positions. I am now a network administrator. I support over 100 users with technical PC/LAN support. The best part of my job is working and learning new technology constantly. The worst is that there are never any "lows" in support. I'm always busy.

My major relates to what I do now when I use my knowledge to create applications to support office functions. My job requires patience, technical knowledge, and communications skills. I would take more classes in programming and possibly go into computer science if I could do it all over again.

The advice I have for students selecting a major is decide what things are fun and go into that area. Take general liberal arts and sciences classes first so you can switch easily to business or computer science if you decide to.

David Shroder, Illinois Institute of Technology, B.S. 1980 Major: Architecture Minor: Computer Science

I chose this major because I liked the feeling of designing and building something that I could point to and say, "I built that." There is a satisfaction there that cannot be found in many things these days.

I have been the manager of software development for a company that builds video display systems for airlines and airports around the world. I design and write the software that communicates the changes for various flight information to the displays as well as directing the activities of several other programmers. The best part of my job is that I get to be involved in the day-to-day running of a small company, and to see a product grow from an idea to hardware running at a customer's site. The worst are the emergencies. Our customers expect us to be available 24 hours a day, seven days a week. It can be a drain sometimes, especially with a very small group like we have.

Architecture taught me how to build very large things. This can be translated to the building of computer systems and products. Of all the things I learned in school, the ability to think "in the large" was probably the most useful. My job requires creativity, flexibility, analytical thinking, and patience.

In many ways, my career to this point has not been anything like I expected when I started college. However, I've been fortunate in being able to use the skills I developed there. Maybe not in the way I expected, but all things considered I would only change decisions I made about jobs, not about college, if given the chance.

My advice to students is to find something that will keep you interested and learning after you leave college. If what you know gets you a job, but you don't enjoy it, there isn't much point to it no matter how much money you make. Also, employers these days often look for attitude and problem-solving skills more than specific knowledge.

Renee Ortbals, Miami University, B.A. 1994 Majors: Marketing and Media Management; Minor: American Literature

I chose this major because it was interesting, it required some creativity, Miami had a strong program as far as the job market is concerned, they had great classes and special programs (i.e., an advertising practicum with real client, budget, and international programs). I have been a sales consultant for two years. I work with college faculty to persuade them to use one of my textbooks in their classes. I also search for possible text authors and reviewers. The best part of my job is working with intelligent, proactive customers who take a vested interest in their classes. The worst is working with challenges in the industry relating to used book buyers, used textbooks, and professional copies being sold to book buyers for cash. My major comes into play when I contribute information to the company regarding trends in each discipline and the industry as a whole—I am constantly conducting market research (focus groups, verbal surveys) and monitoring consumer behavior. It's terrific because in many ways, I can see the value of my major.

My job requires an assertive, personable nature, a strong product knowledge and the ability to recall and disseminate large amounts of information, strong organizational skills, discipline (I work alone out of my home), and autonomy.

I also love the concept of biology, and was a strong science student in high school and college. My biggest challenge has always been that I am a good student in many subjects, but a master of none. Marketing served my interests best, but I do wonder sometimes if I should be teaching literature or biology.

Too many of my peers (and family) regarded choosing a major as a secondary concern. They had no focus or real interest until it seemed to be too late. Unfortunately, the current structures of universities and general (or specific) requirements do not allow students to explore a variety of possible majors—unless, of course, the student wants to invest five or six years. My advice would then be to really focus your efforts on narrowing down a list of majors before entering college with the goal of declaring one freshman year. Sounds simple, but I have so many friends who did not take this approach.

Joseph Chin,
Wesleyan University
Major: College of
Social Studies (CSS)

I chose CSS because it provides a unique approach to learning that complements my interests perfectly. CSS is an interdisciplinary program consisting of government, economics, history, and philosophy. It's a three-year major, beginning in the sophomore year. To enroll, students must submit an application to the college and participate in an interview during the spring semester of their freshman year.

CSS is fondly known as the College of Suicidal Sophomores by Wesleyan students due to its infamous workload. It was this prestigious and daunting reputation that first drew my attention.

I have no definitive career objectives at this point, and ironically, the integration of disciplines, cultivation of a strong work habit, and prestigious reputation is the ideal major for my lack of focus. CSS demands first and foremost a willingness to work. "Any means necessary" is the motto of a CSS major the night before a paper is due. CSS is also grounded in discussion and discourse. Classes are intentionally limited to 10 to 20 students.

CSS has made an effort in recent years to address criticisms of its curriculum. CSS has been attacked as

Eurocentric and male-biased. While all of academia can be criticized for the latter, CSS does tend to obey the traditional teaching approach of English colleges and universities. The reading list resembles that of Columbia's "Great Books" curriculum and the small, discussion-based tutorials have their roots in the classroom settings of Cambridge and Oxford. Still, such criticisms apply only to the sophomore year. During the junior and senior years, independent study and more personal topics are the objectives for CSS majors. Recently, college tutors have also made a concerted effort to integrate feminist theory into their classes.

David Simmons, Bowdoin College, B.A. 1996 Majors: German and Religion

I feel that I didn't really "choose" these majors; the majors chose me. In my sophomore year in high school my family hosted an exchange student from Germany and I began to study German; after graduating from high school I spent a year with that student and his family in northern Germany, not far from Kiel. Although I had taken two years in high school, I could not speak much German at all when I first arrived, but over the course of the year I became quite fluent. When I matriculated at Bowdoin in the fall of 1992, the German department placed me in a 300-level German literature course, which required reading literature and writing analytical papers in German.

I was not entirely satisfied with a single major, however; German almost seemed to be cheating since I already spoke the language. In my first year, I took introductory courses in anthropology, sociology, and religion. Religion 101 was by far the most exciting of these. It was a well-designed course, a little off-beat, and the professor was excellent. The following semester I signed up for a first-year seminar on the book of Job. I was amazed by this seminar, and did quite well. The professor, who taught courses in Judaism, Christianity, and Bible, persuaded me in the most positive terms to continue with religion.

The most difficult part of the German major was producing original, creative thought in a second language and communicating it both verbally and in writing. For religion, it is being able to identify and understand religious behavior in cultures that are often extravagantly different from our own, and writing about religious patterns and activity in relationship to broader cultural contexts without sounding like a flake.

The German major requires proficiency in the language, of course, but also the ability to read critically and write intelligently. Religion demands open-mindedness and sensitivity, prerequisites for studying religions that sometimes seem bizarre, and an ability to place details into a larger picture that explains how humans relate to their universe in a religious metaphor. The ability to analyze shrewdly and write clearly is also essential.

People assume that all religion majors are theologians with plans for the ministry, which is absurdly untrue. Sometimes people become confessional around us and feel it necessary to explain that they haven't gone to church recently or are lapsed Catholics, or secular Jews, or whatever. We have to be very patient as we explain that the study of religion is not restricted to either Christianity or God. Religion majors are probably the most diverse group of individuals with different backgrounds and interests that I can think of, but sadly the stereotype is perpetuated by people who are stuck in a religious rut. Religion majors are an interesting breed. My personal feeling is that students are drawn to the study of religion because they have had some moment of "enlightenment" in which they came to question what they had been taught about religion by their own traditions. Many of them feel marginalized by the major traditions, and seek meaningful alternatives. Nearly all of them, I believe, have some kind of personal commitment to a certain area of religious expression that becomes the focus of their studies.

Sean Makens,
Colorado School of
Mines
Major: Metallurgy
and Materials
Science Engineering

This major provides me with a balance between the disciplines at CSM. The course work includes physics, chemistry, engineering, geology, etc. The major also provides a balance between theory and practical applications. I was attracted by its broadness.

The hardest part of my major was deciding what part I was the most interested in, and developing that part. Whether I was to focus on extractive, production, or materials research had a definite impact on my different career paths.

I intend to work in the industry for the first few years in the production side of the field.

Dana Levine,
Goucher College,
B.A. 1993
Major: International
Relations

I love to travel and enjoyed my political science as well as history classes and found that this major incorporated most of what I was looking for at the time.

I am now executive assistant to Ambassador Donald McHenry. I have held this position in addition to working for the Development Office at the Georgetown School of Foreign Service for a year and a half. My responsibilities include those of correspondence, incoming gift maintenance, scheduling reinstatements, events planning for donors, parents, and alumni as well as interaction with students, state department, and corporate boards. For the most part it was on-the-job learning and what was "required" was organizational skills and confidence to make executive decisions.

The best part of my job is the contacts I am making and the environment in which I am working. My major relates very little to what I do now. I am lucky enough to have the opportunity to ask the Ambassador about current and world events, so I am continuing to grow and learn.

In giving advice to undergraduates I would most definitely major in something that didn't necessarily matter or connect to a job. Liberal arts education is important and crucial in terms of being a more well-rounded, interesting individual. History and philosophy would have had more to offer in terms of having a base knowledge of skills and education. It is important to make yourself marketable, because keep in mind that most jobs/careers have "on-the-job" training. Analytical skills are crucial and will certainly help you go a long way in any career. Many times at a graduate level career paths or choice will differ from those thought of or pursued at the onset of an undergraduate level. Jobs and experiences help formulate better decisions in terms of career goals.

Mari Philipsborn,
Washington
University, 1992
Major: Anthropology

I chose anthropology for exposure to diversity and global cultures. Today, I'm assistant director of fundraising and corporate development at Rush–Presbyterian St. Luke's Medical Center. The best part of the job is cultivating relationships with donors and researching people and projects. My major is directly related to what I do now because in some subfields of anthropology you study people and cultures and how they operate complex systems and sets of symbols. In some ways it is similar to what I do now. Some skills are directly relevant—writing, listening, observing.

The main skills my job requires are communication, both verbal and written, listening to understand people, and negotiation. If I had it to do all over again I would have taken a more rounded load freshman year and not entered the premed program, which was all science.

I'd advise students to find something that fascinates you. Don't be afraid to ask lots of questions and be demanding of your teachers and yourself! Don't deny yourself a liberal arts education.

Scott Stoddard, Gettysburg College, 1990 Major: Political Science

My title is Account Manager for Deluxe Financial Services. Primarily I sell checks and related financial forms to the banking industry. Ironically, my major does not seemingly relate to what I do now. However the liberal arts education, of which political science courses were a part, helped foster many skills that I use daily. Namely, the ability to communicate on a higher level via written correspondence, oral communication, and problem solving.

In using a bicycle as an analogy, my job involves two sets of skills. The front wheel of the bicycle represents people skills, while the back wheel represents technical and product knowledge. Like the wheels of a bicycle, the people skills or the front wheel comes first and then the rear wheel or production knowledge follows. Both are equally important for the bicycle or for the job to roll along.

The best part of my job is meeting with customers to introduce new products and helping to ensure that their bank is running a profitable check program. The worst part is handling service issues and administrative paperwork.

Up until you choose your major, sample as many different types of classes as possible. Try to minor in something as well. If offered the chance to take electives, diversify and take classes outside of your "comfort zone." Having to do it again, I would have also supplemented a diverse curriculum with more business and computer courses.

Chris Kalwett, Northern Illinois University, 1996 Major: Engineering Technology

I chose my major because it is more "hands-on" than mechanical or electrical engineering. In my job as a manufacturing engineer I find ways to improve productivity, efficiency, quality, ergonomics, and overall manufacturing. My job is most satisfying because many of the things I improve are noticeable soon after implementation.

There are a wide variety of skills that help me every day. They include an overall knowledge of modern manufacturing principles, solid understanding of mechanics, machines, and tooling, and computer proficiency—most modern machinery is computer controlled. Lastly, despite having a technical job, communication skills are essential.

My major relates almost one hundred percent to what I do now. Many of the principles and practices I learned relate to everyday projects.

Try to picture yourself at 35 or 40 years of age, and think about where you want to be. I know you are supposed to study what you enjoy, but many majors will not yield a salary that will raise a family.

Chris Sciora,
Rensselaer
Polytechnic Institute,
1989
Major: Computer
Science

My lifelong love of computers and graphics carried me through my college career and to starting my own company, Chronologic Corp. My major is intimately interwoven into daily activities because our company runs entirely through computers.

A simple answer to what I do in my career is everything. I most enjoy sales and growth but also handle accounting, marketing, and development. One skill that is essential in my position is vision, or having a creative goal.

If I could do it all over again I would have borrowed money to get started and skipped the first two years on a shoestring.

My advice would be to find something you enjoy and realize it does not have to be, and probably won't be, a lifelong decision. You can always change your career.

Greg Zonca,
University of
Michigan at Ann
Arbor
Major: Mechanical
Engineering

I am soon to finish my major in mechanical engineering. Important questions I would ask myself when choosing a major or a department or a class are: Will I be able to get sufficient help with questions that arise in homework and for preparing for tests? and, What kind of teaching style does the professor have?

Just recently I have begun the search for a permanent job after graduation. Soon I will embark on the wonderful world of travel paid by companies that are looking to hire me for their companies for the future. My advice for people looking for jobs is to first get an internship or co-op. Build relationships and get a feel for real engineering.

Use the placement office on campus and find your friends. Call them. Talk to your parents and their friends. Use trade journals to get company names and numbers.

Katherine Lorscheider, Duke University Major: Economics

I was originally interested in accounting, but switched my focus to organizational structure and design. Economics is also very good for teaching you a way of thinking that is relevant to a real-world environment.

Taking courses that are relevant to jobs other than being an economist is the hardest part of this major. At other schools, you can get a business or an accounting degree, but here, you need to specialize within economics so that your area of knowledge is not too broad.

I plan on going into management consulting after graduation, and possibly business school in a few years.

Ceres Chua, Emory University Majors: Biology and Chemistry

Ever since I took my first biology class in high school, I knew that biology was a subject I wanted to pursue. After taking additional courses in college, it became very clear to me that it was what I wanted to do. As for my chemistry major, I decided to study it out of convenience. I only needed to take two more classes after all of the chemistry that satisfied biology prerequisites to complete the major.

There is nothing in particular that's hard about my biology major, except that the subject is too dynamic. It is an ever-changing field, so one is required to keep up with it, especially when engaged in research. The hardest part about my chemistry major is physical chemistry. It is impossible to understand.

Hopefully, I will be attending medical school after graduation. If everything works out nicely, I will be taking a year off to pursue research with the National Institute of Health before continuing with my academics.

Lisa Huffhines, University of Texas at Arlington Major: Nursing

I chose nursing for its flexibility and versatility—flexible work hours and versatile positions, locations, and opportunities for advancement. It is a career, not a job. Nursing changes roles as health care changes routes of delivery.

The hardest part of studying nursing is the many hours put into book work as well as clinical hours. The full-time student (12 to 15 hours) will be busy Monday through

Friday, 8:00 A.M. to 5:00 P.M. That makes it difficult to work much.

After graduation I hope to get into oncology (cancer) nursing and emergency department nursing for the first year at the local hospital. I plan to enter graduate school next year for family nurse practitioner.

Jennifer Shaw,
University of Illinois
at Chicago, B.A. 1996
Major: English

I went to a college preparatory high school at which we were strongly encouraged to have a major chosen as early as junior year. Having little information at hand, and certainly not enough life experience, I chose Occupational Therapy at the ripe age of seventeen. UIC was the only school in the state with the program, so that's where I went.

The first year was just general education, a lot of psychology, some biology. But when it came time to register for my sophomore year—the year I would need two consecutive anatomy classes, I found the one and only anatomy class of 500 seats was closed. Oh well, I thought, I guess I'll have to take it next year. But the next year, it was closed, and I wondered why in the world at such a big school (and one with so many medical professions, for that matter) would they offer only one anatomy class per semester? I assumed my advisor could somehow overenroll me, so I went to see him, totally unprepared for the reaming I was to receive regarding my grades. He told me in no uncertain terms that Bs and Cs are not acceptable, and I need not bother applying to the OT program, because I would not be accepted. He even went on to suggest that I see a counselor if I'd been having any personal problems. I sat there, paralyzed, wondering if I would cry first or throw a punch his way for even suggesting that I had problems. I didn't say a word, I just nodded when he told me to change my major.

Don't get me wrong, I will always despise that man for treating me the way he did, but he was right. The OT program wasn't for me. Not with those grades. The truth was, I had made that choice too early, and knew nothing about it. So I took a serious look at what I had been doing in school, and how I had been doing, when I noticed a peculiar pattern. I had nearly flunked all tests, and aced all papers. Sure, it evened out to a nice, round C, but that was when I realized that I had a talent for writing. Yes, I thought. Why not just write? So I quickly changed my major to English, and began getting As and the occasional B (in electives in other disciplines, of course).

There's no doubt in my mind that I made the right decision. I have one huge advantage over all other liberal arts and sciences graduates: I can write. And I don't mean just term papers or poetry or fiction or nonfiction. Writing is so much more than that. It's quick comprehension, it's a love of words, it's creativity.

Sure, there are stereotypes of English majors. But they don't bother me as much as the questions I've answered a million times or more. "What are you going to do with an English degree?" "So you're going to teach?" And I swear, I've heard this one at least five times, "How can you major in your own native language?" Over the years you manage to come up with some snappy comebacks. It's all part of belonging to that "useless" major. As far as jobs go, I'm looking into editing, publishing, public relations, advertising, marketing, journalism, anything, really. I've only been out of school for two weeks, just give me some time.

The best advice I can give students is to not declare anything for the first two years unless you absolutely have to. If you look at any college handbook, the general requirements are pretty much the same anywhere you go, so you can see what you like and fulfill those requirements at the same time. Neat trick, huh? Oh, and of course, pick something that interests you (although I don't know many people who pick things that don't interest them). And be honest with yourself. If you're not doing so well in what you picked, ask yourself if you really wanted to do it in the first place. If it is, then you'd better get to work, and if not, then you have to find out what you can do. Sometimes change is good.

Tracey Holloway
Brown University,
1995
Major: Applied
Mathematics

When I began college, I thought I would major in history or political science. The rather drastic switch to applied math occurred through a series of trials and errors. First semester, I took two classes in the humanities/social sciences and two in math/physical sciences. The science classes were primarily to keep open the premed option, which was the most "sciency" career I'd considered. However, I loved first-year chemistry, and enjoyed math more than I ever had in high school. Many of my friends that first year planned on majoring in science, and I began to consider this idea as well. After some thought, I decided to try engineering, which seemed to combine creativity and science in the design process. One semester of that program, however, turned me off to engineering as my science field of choice. (I felt it was too dry, and much less creative than other branches of science, contrary to my initial hope. In retrospect, I think that engineering actually could be quite enjoyable, but that initial course did not succeed in convincing me at the time.) Sophomore year, I took a course in linear algebra, which I loved, and it convinced me that higher mathematics offered my desired blend of creativity and problem solving. Concurrently, I took an economics class, which I also liked, and decided that by majoring in applied mathematics, I could pursue both math and economics. Although I ended up focusing on fluid dynamics (an active research area in the applied math department) rather than economics in later years of college, the choice to major in applied math was motivated by a desire to combine economics with mathematics.

Now I am a second year graduate student at Princeton University in the Atmospheric and Oceanic Sciences Program, working on my Ph.D. During the first two years of the program we take classes and begin research. After the spring of our second year, we concentrate exclusively on research. A great deal of work at my lab is studying the dynamics of the atmosphere and oceans with mathematical models that are run on computers.

The best part of this work is that I am being paid to do exactly what I want to do—I get to choose a research project of interest to me, and most classes offer freedom to work on projects that I choose. The worst part is so much work to do and there is never really time off. The weekends and evenings, during which time many of my non-student friends get to relax guilt-free, are important times to study or work on research.

Graduate study in math requires a strong math and physics background, good programming skills, and self-discipline to work on research/classes without constant deadlines or close supervision.

If I had it to do all over again, part of me wants to say, "take more physics or other classes that would directly benefit my present work," but in other ways I am happy to have had the broad background I gained in college, since now I'm working exclusively on science.

My advice to those choosing a major is to give a lot of thought to what would make you really happy and excited to do in the long run, and try to learn how the career you want ties back into classes you could take. Then, think of what other careers this major would prepare you for if you change your mind or can't get your ideal position.

Although there are not that many astronauts in the world, preparing for a "dream job" like that would prepare you for other related jobs, whether in the space program, or as a scientific researcher, or as a pilot, or as a science teacher.

I'd say, prepare for your ultimate job, but try to keep other options open as long as possible.

Wai-Sinn Chan
Yale University, 1996
Major: Psychology

Freshman year I was considering eighteen different majors (OK, five seriously). First semester it had narrowed down to five, second semester down to one. I really enjoyed introductory psych so I took more upper-level courses, which led me to the major.

I really had no idea what I wanted to do in the future and based my decision on good classes and professors more than other more practical considerations, i.e., what are you going to do with that? Psychology is a broad field so I could really dabble in my different interests.

Although a typical psych paper is very structured and has less room for creativity, I really learned how to write a solid APA (American Psychological Association) style paper. More creative papers such as experiment proposals and my senior essay were good exercises in problem solving. These are skills useful for many jobs in market research. I will especially need to be able to put problem-solving and writing skills to use. Today I work for an advertising agency and use my research, analytical, and writing skills.

If I had it to do all over again I would try to focus more within the major into more directly related fields like marketing or into graduate school. I enjoyed the freedom of the major but would have preferred more of a focus. I would also have considered double majoring more seriously. Also, taking interdisciplinary courses such as sociology and education was also valuable.

I'd advise undergraduates to talk to everyone you can, upperclasspeople to find out what courses and professors they recommend, professors and teaching assistants to find out more about their own experiences and suggestions. Profs will be able to describe grad school in excruciating detail. Job-hunting seniors will be able to tell you how useful your degree is. Also valuable is talking to professionals outside of academia. I'd learn about career paths early on.

**Linda Lee
Cornell University,
1996
Major: Chemical
Engineering**

You must enjoy your major. Don't expect actual jobs to be the direct application of what you learned in classes. I've been an engineer for four months, doing products research, concept development, consumer understanding, in-market learning, etc. My major taught me critical thinking and problem solving. The best part of my job is that I interact with many functions, get a better "big" picture that way.

**Patrick Priore
University of Illinois
at Chicago, 1990
Major: English**

When I think about it now, I never for a minute went to college to master a trade or train for a job. I just wanted to have fun and meet cool people, which I did. I knew before my first day at orientation that I would be an English major. It was what I knew I already enjoyed most about school and it offered the most variety. Plus, I wasn't as good at anything else. Today, I work in San Francisco as a buyer for the Gap and travel to the Far East several times a year. My writing and communication skills definitely give me a competitive edge in memo writing, negotiations, presentations, etc.

Go with your gut is my advice. Don't force yourself into a course of study that is tedious or boring. It should be fun and excite you.

**Scott Facher
Dartmouth College,
B.A. 1990
Major: Theater**

I chose theater because I loved reading plays. I found myself drawn to certain professors in these departments. But mostly, when it was time to choose a major my passions were outside the classroom. My love for acting had started to grow. I loved to play the violin. I loved my friends in college. In college there were a million things I wanted to be doing when I wasn't in class. Reading assignments weren't usually among them. But there were moments reading a play or novel where I wouldn't have wanted to be anywhere else. I've called myself an actor since graduation, six years ago. I got my first paying job doing summer stock right out of college. The best part of my job is the acting, all of it. Rehearsing, an actor is like a psychologist or archeologist, exploring the human psyche, finding the connection between ourselves and others—an actor is also an archeologist of the human mind and spirit.

Don't worry so much about "what will help you when you graduate." Maybe if you know early on that you have a passion for sciences or for economics, then focusing there could help you in your post-graduation plans. But with anything else, as far as I can see, you can do anything with any major. What a liberal arts education teaches you is how to learn and how to think. What you really need in the "real world" is something to show when you walk in the door. However you can do that will be fine. So major in what you are passionate about.

Shannon Shean Sonoma State University, B.A. 1992 Major: Psychology

I picked my major because I enjoyed a psychology class in high school and working with the career counselor there. Today I work for a pharmaceutical benefit manager providing administrative support. Once I get into sales my degree may come in handy.

My mistake in college was not researching social work fully, the field I was interested in. I would have discovered there's a big commitment as far as education goes and then the pay is not competitive. Research the field you're interested in, talk to people who currently perform in this field. Get a sense of how competitive it is and what the job satisfaction level is.

Jessica M. Schindhelm, Bowdoin College Major: Women's Studies

I think the hardest part of my major is defending it to others. People are always asking me "What can you do with a women's studies major?" I usually reply with something like, "What can you do with a liberal arts degree regardless of the major?" I mean today's job market really doesn't cater to those who don't have work experience or a graduate degree. For the past two school years and over this summer I have been working at Bowdoin's Office of Communications in the Publications department. I think publications is something I could go into after college. I definitely have a lot of experience now.

My major more fits into my attitude than my career. It has given me an outlook on life that allows me to question the standards and perhaps to open some closed minds. Of course there are stereotypical images with this major as with every major. I think that the most harmful of these is the "angry young woman" or "lesbian." I personally don't mind being called either because if I don't validate people's claims, then they are no longer harmful. But I do think that it prevents many men from taking these classes or accepting this major because it puts a stigma on them, which very few men are willing to accept. I don't think that the stereotypes are true completely, although there is some truth to every stereotype. What is harmful is when people don't look past the stereotype and actually listen to ideas.

Jason Black, Michigan State University Major: Urban Forestry

I originally went to the University of Oklahoma to major in meteorology. I came to that decision because even as a young boy I would stay up late to watch the extended forecast on the late news. I was fascinated by the extremes, cold, hot, but most of all big storms (snow, tornadoes, etc.). Unfortunately, after two years of school I realized that I just did not have the mathematical skills to proceed through the program. After that I was at a total loss as to what my major should be. After three or four weeks and at my father's urging, I gave advertising a try. My father, his new wife, and all their friends were in the advertising field and I had grown up all around it. Unfortunately, that was disastrous. I decided to quit school and work where I had the previous summers for the Streets/ Forestry Department doing tree trimming, planting, and removals. After working there for one and a half years I realized that forestry, particularly urban forestry, was for me. I felt rather stupid that it had taken me this long to realize this because as a small boy I was always trimming the trees and shrubs in the neighborhood as well as at my relatives when we went to visit. I chose urban forestry because I couldn't imagine being on a mountaintop out west in a national park. The city was too important a part of me to move away from. I also realized how important the environment was to me, not only maintaining it but improving and protecting it from outside interests but also from the natural pests and dangers that threaten our nation's forests.

Because an urban forester generally works for a city or state government, much more of his or her time is spent dealing with the public. Public relations courses are required in the curriculum.

The advice I'd give is you shouldn't cave in to any pressures your friends or family might put on you. Don't feel that you must know what you want to major in immediately upon enrollment in college. You'll be much happier in life if you stay true to your heart and do what makes you happy.

Check Out the Professional Associations

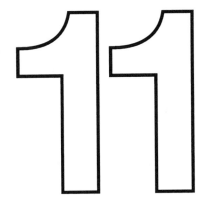

Professional associations have a vested interest in providing information to students. Informing students about the benefits and particulars of their profession ensures a continuing supply of people in the next generations to carry on their work, and pay dues.

Ask the associations for the following kinds of information:

1. people in your geographic area who are willing to give informational interviews

2. internship and volunteer opportunities for finding out more about the profession

3. scholarships available for students studying in the association's field

4. the latest statistics on salaries and job projections

5. packets of information on the variety of jobs held in

this profession, education required, and the outlook
for the profession in the future.

A number of national organizations provide information
and materials to students interested in particular fields.
Some of these national associations are listed here, with
Internet address when available. Visit their Web sites,
call, or write for information on fields that are of interest
to you.

Accountant
American Accounting Association
5717 Bessie Dr.
Sarasota, FL 34233-2399
(941) 921-7747
www.rutgers.edu/acct/raw/aaa/aaa/html

Anthropologist
American Anthropological Association
4350 N. Fairfax Dr., Suite 640
Arlington, VA 22203
(703) 528-1902
www.ameranthassn.org

Architect
American Institute of Architects
1735 New York Ave. NW
Washington, DC 20006
(202) 626-7300
www.aia.org

Artist
American Artists Professional League
c/o Salmagundi Club
47 Fifth Ave.
New York, NY 10003
(212) 645-1345

Author/Writer
National Writer's Association
1450 S. Havana, Suite 424
Aurora, CO 80012
(303) 751-7844

Banker
    American Banker's Association
        1120 Connecticut Ave. NW
        Washington, DC 20036
        (202) 663-5000
        www.aba.com

Biologist
    American Institute of Biological Sciences
        730 Eleventh St. NW
        Washington, DC 20001-4521
        (202) 628-1500
        www.aibs.org

Broker
    New York Stock Exchange
        11 Wall St.
        New York, NY 10005
        (212) 656-3000
        www.nyse.com

Chemist
    American Chemical Society
        1155 16th St. NW
        Washington, DC 20036
        (202) 872-4600
        www.acs.org

Communications
    National Communications Association
        16 E. 34th St., 15th Floor
        New York, NY 10016
        (212) 683-8585

Computer Programmer
    Association for Computing Machinery
        1515 Broadway
        New York, NY 10036-5701
        (212) 869-7440
        www.acm.org

Criminologist
> National Criminal Justice Association
> 444 N. Capitol St. NW, Suite 618
> Washington, DC 20001
> (202) 347-4900

Dietician
> American Dietetic Association
> 216 W. Jackson Blvd., Suite 800
> Chicago, IL 60606-6995
> (312) 899-1739

Economist
> American Economic Association
> 2014 Broadway, Suite 305
> Nashville, TN 37203-2418
> (615) 322-2595
> www.vanderbilt.edu/AEA

Educator
> American Educational Studies Association
> Educational Policy Studies Dept., University Plaza
> Georgia State University
> Atlanta, GA 30303
> (404) 651-2582

Engineer
> National Society of Professional Engineers
> 1420 King St.
> Alexandria, VA 22314-2794
> (703) 684-2800

Engineer, Civil
> American Society of Civil Engineers
> c/o Natalie Soulier
> 1015 15th St. NW, Suite 600
> Washington, DC 20005
> (202) 789-2200
> www.asce.org

Geographer

American Geographical Society
156 Fifth Ave., Suite 600
New York, NY 10010-7002
(212) 422-5456

Geologist

American Geological Institute
4220 King St.
Alexandria, VA 22302
(703) 379-2480
www.agiweb.org

Historian

American Historical Association
400 A St. SE
Washington, DC 20003
(202) 544-2422

Language Specialist

American Association of Language Specialists
1000 Connecticut Ave. NW, Suite 9
Washington, DC 20036
(301) 986-1542

Lawyer

American Bar Association
750 N. Lake Shore Dr.
Chicago, IL 60611
(312) 988-5000
www.abanet.org

Marketing

American Marketing Association
250 S. Wacker Dr., Suite 200
Chicago, IL 60606
(312) 648-0536
www.ama.org

Management
American Management Association
135 W. 50th St.
New York, NY 10020
(212) 586-8100
www.amanet.org

Mathematics
American Mathematical Society
P.O. Box 6248
Providence, RI 02940
(401) 455-4000
www.ams.org

Musician
National Association of Schools of Music
11250 Roger Bacon Dr., Suite 21
Reston, VA 22090
www.nasm.org

Oceanographer
National Association of Marine Surveyors
P.O. Box 9306
Chesapeake, VA 23321-9306
(800) 822-6267
www.namsurveyors.org

Pharmacist
American Pharmaceutical Association
2215 Constitution Ave. NW
Washington, DC 20037
(202) 628-4410

Philosopher
American Philosophical Society
104 S. Fifth St.
Philadelphia, PA 19106-3387
(215) 440-3400

Physician
> Council on Medical Education
> American Medical Association
> 515 N. State St.
> Chicago, IL 60610
> (312) 464-4804
> www.ama-assn.org

Political Science
> American Political Science Association
> 1527 New Hampshire Ave. NW
> Washington, DC 20036
> (202) 483-2512

Psychologist
> American Psychological Association
> 750 First St. NE
> Washington, DC 20002-4242
> (202) 336-5500
> www.apa.org

Public Relations
> International Public Relations Association—U.S.
> Chapter
> 18 Loveton Cir.
> P.O. Box 6000
> Sparks, MD 21152-6000
> (410) 435-7642

Sociologist
> American Sociological Association
> 1722 N St. NW
> Washington, DC 20036
> (202) 833-3410

Theater
> American Alliance for Theatre and Education
> P.O. Box 873411
> Dept. of Theatre
> Arizona State University
> Tempe, AZ 85287-3411
> (602) 965-6064

Famous People and Their Majors

Lee Iacocca graduated from Lehigh University in Bethlehem, PA, in 1945 with a degree in industrial engineering. He goes back to his alma mater often to teach and help with the Iacocca Institute, a program focused on teaching competitiveness in business on two fronts—the classroom and the factory floor.

Warren Littlefield, president of NBC Entertainment, graduated from Hobart College in Geneva, NY, in 1976 with an English major.

Musician John Mellencamp received an associate's degree in broadcasting in 1973 from Vincennes University in Indiana.

Dan Rather graduated in 1953 with a degree in journalism from Sam Houston State Teachers College.

Musician Chris Isaak was an English major at the University of the Pacific in Stockton, CA. He also spent a year studying abroad in Japan. He has said he fell into music because he couldn't make it right away as a writer. Actress Janet Leigh majored in music therapy at University of the Pacific. Jazz legend Dave Brubeck, another University of the Pacific alumnus, switched from preveterinary to music after the biology department reportedly told him to major in what he really cared about.

Retired U.S. Navy Captain Dan Brandenstein graduated from the University of Wisconsin at River Falls with degrees in physics and mathematics. Brandenstein retired from the Navy and from NASA in 1994 after serving as the First Astronaut—the chief of NASA's training office. He flew on four space shuttle missions and had the most shuttle hours at the time of his retirement. His hallmarks included serving as the first pilot for a night launch of a space shuttle and he was commander for the maiden voyage of the Columbia.

Actor John Heard graduated from Clark University in Worcestor, MA with a degree in history.

Actor Paul Newman graduated from Kenyon College in 1949 with a degree in drama. Novelist E. L. Doctorow also graduated from Kenyon College with a degree in philosophy in 1952. Fellow alumnus Bill Watterson, cartoonist (Calvin and Hobbes), received a degree in political science in 1980 from Kenyon. Chemist Carl Djerassi, inventor of the birth control pill, received his degree in chemistry from Kenyon in 1943, and political cartoonist Jim Borgman, a Pulitzer Prize winner, graduated with an art major in 1976.

Richard Nixon graduated from Whittier College in 1934 with a history major.

Baseball player Carl Yastrzemski majored in marketing at Merrimack College in North Andover, MA.

Several musicians, including Melissa Etheridge, Steve Smith, Branford Marsalis, and Kevin Eubanks were music majors at Berklee College of Music in Boston, the largest college of music in the world.

Carnegie Mellon's College of Fine Arts has several famous alumni. Stephen Bochco, producer of TV hits "Hill Street Blues," "L.A. Law," "Murder One," and "NYPD Blue" majored in theater there, as did John Wells ("ER"), Oscar winner Holly Hunter, Ted Danson ("Cheers," "Ink"), Jack Klugman ("The Odd Couple"), Blair Underwood ("L.A. Law"), Albert Brooks ("Broadcast News"), Rene Aubnerjonois ("Star Trek, The Next Generation"), Ming-Na Wen ("The Single Guy," "ER," "The Joy Luck Club"), and Barbara Bosson ("Hill Street Blues").

Actor George Wendt, who played Norm on "Cheers," got

his degree in economics from Rockhurst College in Kansas City, MO.

Actor Shawn Christian, who plays tough mechanic Mike Kasnoff on the soap opera "As the World Turns," graduated from Ferris State University in 1989 with a marketing degree.

Gordon Jump, the actor who played on "WKRP in Cincinnatti" and who is now known as the lonely Maytag repairman on the brand name's TV commercials, graduated from Kansas State University with a degree in journalism.

Chris Farley of "Saturday Night Live" fame, as well as the movies *Tommy Boy* and *Black Sheep*, is a 1986 graduate of Marquette University with a degree in performing arts. Other Marquette grads include Anthony Crivello, broadway actor and singer (*Kiss of the Spider Woman*) with a performing arts degree in 1978; Pat Finn, comedian/actor ("George Wendt Show," "Murphy Brown"), 1987 interpersonal communication graduate; and the president of the Green Bay Packers, Robert Harlan, in 1958 with a degree in journalism. "Benny the Bull" is Dan Lemonnier, who received his degree in speech from Marquette in 1978. He runs a business called Folksongs and Foolery Entertainment.

Thomas Alva Edison received his bachelor of science in applied science and technology from Thomas Edison State College in Trenton, NJ, in 1992. Edison received an earned degree, albeit posthumously, thanks to the critical evaluations of College assessment staff and the meticulous scholarship of the Rutgers University "Edison Papers" faculty, who compiled portfolios of Edison's writings that documented his college-level learning in a wide range of fields. Edison's great-grandson, Barry Sloane, accepted the degree for his great-grandfather during commencement ceremonies in October 1992. To Edison State College's knowledge, the degree awarded to Thomas Edison is the only earned degree awarded posthumously for demonstration of college-level knowledge acquired outside the classroom.

Comedian George Wallace, a favorite of comedy clubs and late-night TV talk shows, graduated from the University of Akron in 1972 with a degree in marketing.

Julia Louis-Dreyfus, the irrepressible Elaine on "Seinfeld," earned a B.S. in Speech from Northwestern University in 1982; novelist Saul Bellow earned a B.S. in Sociology in 1937; Richard Gephart of the U.S. Congress received a B.S. in Speech in 1962.

Linda Allard, director of design for Ellen Tracy Fashions, was an art history major at Kent State University, from which she was graduated in 1962. Another famous alum at Kent is Richard Ferry, class of 1959, co-founder and president of Korn-Ferry International, one of the world's largest executive search firms with more than 40 offices around the globe. He was an accounting major.

Annette Sandberg, class of 1993, with majors in law and justice at Central Washington University, is the first woman in the country to head a state policy agency. She supervises the police forces in the state of Washington.

"Mr. Bagel," Murray Lender, graduated from Canopic College in 1950. He is past chairman of Lender's Bagel Bakery, which was founded by his father in 1927. Lender's grew to be the world's largest bagel bakery and was sold to Kraft Foods, which retained him as a spokesperson. His major was business.

C. Jeanne Bowers Shaheen, the first woman to serve as governor of New Hampshire, is a 1969 graduate of Shippensburg University of Pennsylvania. She majored in English. Another English major from Shippensburg, Dean Koontz, internationally known best-selling author, was a 1967 graduate of the school.

U.S. Senator Strom Thurmond (South Carolina) majored in horticulture at Clemson University. He graduated in 1923.

A history major at Nazareth College of Rochester, Class of 1985, Jeff Van Gundy went on to be the coach of the New York Knicks basketball team. He is the youngest coach in the NBA.

Another history major, Dan Moldea, graduated from The University of Akron in 1974, and is now an investigative journalist. His credits include the book *Evidence Disclosed: The Inside Story of the Police Investigation of O.J. Simpson*, which made the *New York Times* bestseller list. His other books include *The Hoffa Wars: Teamsters, Rebels, Politicians and the Mob*, and *The Killing of Robert F. Kennedy: An Investigation of Motive, Means, and Opportunity*.

Alice Rivlin is the assistant director of the Federal Reserve, behind Alan Greenspan. She has a degree in economics (Class of 1952) from Bryn Mawr College.

Richard H. Jones, who received a degree in mathematics in 1972 from Harvey Mudd College, is currently serving as the U.S. Ambassador to Lebanon.

Gloria Steinem graduated from Smith College in 1956 as a government major. She is founder of *Ms.* magazine, the Ms. Foundation for Women, Voters of Choice, and the National Women's Political Caucus. She was the first famous woman to make a point of announcing publicly that she had turned forty.

A Knox College graduate, Dr. Robert F. Spetzler (biology and chemistry, 1967), pioneered the technique of "hypodermic cardiac arrest." In this process the bodies of patients are brought down to near freezing and the lowered temperature gives additional time to perform highly delicate and risky neurosurgical operations. Jimmy Breslin wrote a book about his experience as a neurosurgical patient of Dr. Spetzler.

Burt Rutan, a 1965 aeronautical engineering graduate of the California Polytechnic State University, is in the history books for space travel. In December 1986 he flew nonstop around the earth in nine days in the Voyager, an aircraft he designed and built. It was the first time an aircraft circled the earth without stopping to refuel.

Back in 1891, when a law degree required less than today's major (two years after high school), Judge Kenesaw Mountain Landis, the first commissioner of baseball, was graduated from Northwestern's School of Law.